The Alabama Bomber Boys

*Unlocking Memories of Alabamians
Who Bombed the Third Reich*

Donald E. Wilson

HERITAGE BOOKS
2008

HERITAGE BOOKS
AN IMPRINT OF HERITAGE BOOKS, INC.

Books, CDs, and more—Worldwide

For our listing of thousands of titles see our website
at
www.HeritageBooks.com

Published 2008 by
HERITAGE BOOKS, INC.
Publishing Division
100 Railroad Ave. #104
Westminster, Maryland 21157

Copyright © 2008 Donald E. Wilson

All rights reserved. No part of this book may be reproduced or transmitted in any form or by any means, electronic or mechanical, including photocopying, recording or by any information storage and retrieval system without written permission from the author, except for the inclusion of brief quotations in a review.

International Standard Book Numbers
Paperbound: 978-0-7884-4682-5
Clothbound: 978-0-7884-7265-7

For the veterans of the Alabama Chapter of the

Eighth Air Force Historical Society

Contents

Preface and Acknowledgments   vii

Introduction   xiii

1. December 7, 1941: Lives at the Crossroads   1
2. What was the Eighth Air Force?   14
3. Two Cultures, A Single Objective   29
4. An Uncertain Beginning   51
5. Darkness of Winter, Light of Spring   68
6. Air Superiority   85
7. Evasion, Capture and the Stalag   107
8. Over, at Last   130

Notes   142

Bibliography   152

Index   157

Preface and Acknowledgements

The phone rang at 10:00 on Christmas morning. The chaplain from Hospice informed me that Lawson Corley was dead. Not only was I saddened by the news of Lawson's passing, but also aware of my responsibility of making sure that another remarkable but unpublished story from the World War II generation had not died with him. A few days earlier, Lawson had called me to ask me if he might look at what I had written about him in the draft of this book. When I informed him that I was very busy grading end of term papers from my history classes at Samford University, and would see him after Christmas, Lawson begged me to come as soon as possible. His "cancer had taken its toll," he said, "and after Christmas might be too late."

I realized from the tone of Lawson's voice that my papers could wait. The following day I was at his bedside reading him the story of his life as a bombardier on a B-24 Liberator over Nazi Germany, and his account of the near death he experienced as a prisoner of war in a German prison camp. Lawson smiled when I finished, and his eyes welled up in gratitude as he realized that his story, told orally on so many occasions, would be his legacy to later generations. As we shook hands for the last time, I reflected again on the reasons for this book, and also on the consequences of not recording the stories of a generation of American patriots that is rapidly succumbing to an ever-increasing mortality rate.

The "why" of this book stretches back over the past fifty years and my personal contacts with the history and participants of the American Eighth Air Force of World War II. First, as a young Air Force officer in an Air Evacuation Squadron manned primarily by former Army Air Forces pilots, many of whom had once served in the Eighth Air Force, I listened with admiration and awe to their accounts of bombing missions over Germany and heard stories of unbelievable courage that remain with me to this day. Then in later years my career took me to a faculty assignment in the Department of History at the United States Air Force Academy, where I had the opportunity to study and enter into discussions on the concepts behind long-range strategic bombing in World War II. I also met many of the air pioneers of that crusade, including Generals Ira Eaker, Carl Spaatz, Curtis LeMay, Lauris Norstad and Nathan Twining, to name a few. I was hooked on the subject and especially the personal accounts of its participants.

In a later assignment at the Air Force Historical Research Center at Maxwell Air Force Base in Montgomery, Ala., I had access to the unit records of all Eighth Air Force bomber groups. As I examined official records and air crew reports from legendary bombing missions over targets such as Schweinfurt, Regensburg and Berlin, long associated with grim statistics of losses of men and aircraft, I developed a curiosity as to the airmen behind the numbers, where they came from, and more importantly their experiences as they left training in the United States for the unfamiliar culture in Britain, and the frigid and unforgiving skies over Germany. How did young men, for the most part fresh out of high school, transition from their relatively quiet lives in post-depression America to center stage in an air war in the skies over Europe unlike any in the history of air power?

In recent years I have been privileged to explore further the history of the Eighth Air Force, both in the classroom at Samford as part of my military history courses, and through research in England, where I had the opportunity to travel to the area north and northeast of London called East Anglia, the World War II home to some sixty Eighth Air Force bomber bases. I spent many hours talking to British citizens who lived near the now-deserted air fields and during the war became lifelong friends of the airmen, or as one described them, "me friends." Their accounts of those experiences added reality to the history I had been teaching, and they contributed to a recent travel guide I published, *On the Trail of Patriots in World War II Britain*. But most importantly they provided an insight into the lives and changing experiences of the men of the so-called "friendly invasion," the men of the legendary Eighth Air Force, or as it was appropriately called, the "Mighty Eighth."

Some 350 thousand of the million and a half men who "invaded" Britain beginning in January 1942 flew bomber missions from those hastily constructed air fields. Twenty-six thousand of that number gave their lives in the process. In the six decades since the war in Europe ended, the heroic stories of those airmen have been recorded in hundreds of books, articles, and oral and written memoirs. Many thousands of other accounts are locked in the minds of survivors and unfortunately will never be told. Sadly, with the ranks of World War II veterans decreasing at a rapid rate each day, archivists in libraries, museums and universities are racing against time to record their stories. This book is one such effort, and a daunting task in that all of my subjects are now in their eighties and at least ten of their number have passed away since I began this account.

While my past experiences provided the motivation for a book on the Eighth Air Force, I could not have written it without the help of a very special group of veterans. They are members of the very active Eighth Air Force Historical Society, specifically those in the Alabama chapter. The Society, in a race against the reality of the mortality statistics of the World War II generation, has as its mission the collection of as many accounts of Eighth Air Force veterans as possible, living and dead, and to educate the uninformed, especially young people, on heroics they never knew occurred.

While I was quite familiar with the air war through study of the Eighth, I realized that these men shared accounts I had never heard, accounts that heretofore had been shared only with each other.

I also discovered that within the Alabama chapter the men collectively represented a microcosm of what veterans of the air war from across the nation experienced. Consequently, most of the veterans participating in this book are either natives of Alabama or eventually made Alabama their home. As such, they provided a valuable and accessible resource for this book, and thankfully were more than willing to unlock their memories and assist me in my effort. But unlike the compilation of stand-alone biographies that many other historians have written, or the chronological coverage of the Eighth's many missions, I have endeavored to integrate their accounts into the World War II culture from which they came, the culture in Britain from which they flew, the phases of the bombing missions over Nazi Europe, and finally the world to which they returned when the war ended. While this book is directed at an uninformed reader, my major desire is to give the veterans and their families an account they can pass on to generations that follow.

Of course reliance on personal memories can be fraught with both accurate and inaccurate information and must stand the test of verification. This is especially true in this book where I am using memories some six decades old. While I cannot guarantee the accuracy of every account the veterans shared with me, I have, where possible, crosschecked their stories with those of other veterans who shared their experiences in autobiographies and histories. The *Chronology of the Air War*, produced by the Air Force Historical Research Center of the office of Air Force history, along with the center's complete Eighth Air Force collection were especially helpful. My confidence in many of the personal accounts is further based on the faith I have in the degree of attention to detail of many of the veterans, and with the intensity with which they relate their stories. Such deeply embedded accounts definitely have an aura of credibility about them. However, if in spite of every effort toward verification, errors and/or omissions are found, I assume total responsibility.

I must also comment on another type of omission germane to Eighth Air Force history, and that is my lack of coverage of the role of black airmen. Very simply, segregation policies kept such participation in the Army Air Forces to a minimum, and in bomber crews, nonexistent. In the one success story, a few black Americans known as the Tuskegee Airmen did prove that they belonged, and not just in the segregated air force; these men eventually earned their wings and flew fighter aircraft in the 332nd Fighter Group. They were quite successful and proved their abilities and heroism by supporting bomber operations of the Fifteenth Air Force. However, in spite of their skill as fighter pilots the black Americans were not permitted to become part of the bomber forces in Europe.

Many colleagues, veterans and other individuals contributed to this work, and I am deeply appreciative of their help. I am especially grateful to the veterans throughout Alabama; without their oral and written comments this work would have been impossible. I must give special recognition to the Alabama Eighth Air Force Historical Society and its President Henry Arnold and his wife Amy. The Arnolds were especially valuable in placing the Alabama subjects in the book at my disposal, in addition to providing unwavering support since inception of the project. They also read the completed manuscript and were helpful in giving advice that only those close to the subject could give.

For the purposes of this book I define "Alabamians" in two ways: first are the natives of the state who went to war and returned to make Alabama their permanent home. While I depended on those men for a majority of the accounts in the book, I also relied on the men who came from other states but made Alabama their home after the war. Unfortunately, many Alabamians were part of the Eighth but never settled in the state, and neither the Eighth Air Force Society nor other sources have records of their final home of residence.

I am also grateful to the Samford University History Department and John Mayfield for encouraging my efforts through financial support and by awarding me two sabbatical leaves that were so vital to my research in England. Among my History colleagues, David Vess and Betty Mullins were most helpful in reading the manuscript and making suggestions, while Susan Murphy was always there when computer questions arose or clerical assistance was needed. My granddaughter Megan Riley also contributed in helping me with the intricacies of using the computer. I must give special thanks for the professional assistance of Rebecca Day, who edited the final product and formatted the book for publication.

I must also thank my good friend in the Samford Political Science Department, Bill Collins, for always having a listening ear and word of encouragement and, as a veteran, recognizing the need for more coverage of military history in academia. Elizabeth Wells in the Samford library's Special Collections Department continued her role as one of Alabama's most helpful and gifted research authorities by assisting me in both written research and in a very touching and meaningful oral history from Lawson Corley, so critical in telling the story of those airmen who endured the ordeal in German Stalags.

Finally, and in so many ways most importantly, I must also thank my wife Alleen for her usual support and encouragement and also her skill in proofreading the final product.

Introduction

Some memories are so etched in the human psyche that they take on a life of their own. They span the years from one generation to another. Such were those enjoyed and revered by the British citizens of East Anglia, an area north of London, and their "American cousins" who came some six decades ago to help rescue their war-torn country from the German onslaught that had ravaged their land along with most of Europe. For a brief few years, some three hundred thousand young men of the Eighth Air Force or the "mighty eighth, "as it became known, made their home on some sixty air force bases, and became such a part of the centuries-old culture that they earned the British title "our boys." From late 1942 until the spring of 1945 they joined the British Royal Force in taking the war directly to Hitler's "fortress Europe". This is the story of a few of those young men, the relatively peaceful world they came from, the British lives they touched, the horrific war that cost the lives of twenty-five thousand of their number, and the world they returned to when it ended.

The young men came from every state and every walk of life. They represented families from every occupation and social and economic status, and on that memorable Sunday afternoon, their lives as high school and college students, factory workers, and farmers in small towns and cities across America, were interrupted with events that changed their lives forever. For example, John Hard was waiting tables in Cagle Hall at the University of Illinois when he heard the news. Across the country in Hollywood, California, Samuel Ross had just returned home from church, while Glenn Taylor, a freshman at North Carolina State College, who heard the news from a fellow student, was studying for exams in pre-aeronautical engineering, pursuing an education that was to be put on hold for the following three years. Meanwhile, in Syracuse, New York, Bill Curry was relaxing from his previous day's work in a hardware store where he earned ten cents an hour, and like Bill Thompson, who had Sunday off from his job at the Tennessee Coal and Iron plant in Fairfield, Alabama, heard the news on the radio.

But while they, like thousands of other young men who until that day saw their future confined to a narrow range of occupational possibilities and a lifestyle confined to a geographic area not far removed from their places of birth, they had one thing in common. They were destined to be part of the new dimension of warfare and specifically became members of the newly organized Eighth Air Force.

The Eighth Air Force was activated January 28, 1942, at Savannah, Georgia. Between August 17, 1942, and its first mission against Germany, and its last mission on April 25, 1945, the Mighty Eighth, as it was called, flew 459 days and dropped 696,451 tons of bombs. The men who carried out such missions paid a terrible price, with more than twenty-six thousand of their number dying in unimaginable ways. The men who survived share a camaraderie that only they understand. But they are very proud of the part they played in the air war and are most anxious to share their stories with a world that largely knows nothing of their amazing history.

While the history of this powerful bomber force has been recorded by many historians, and though their oral history accounts are available along with countless biographies and autobiographies, to the average American of recent generations, especially today's students from elementary school through college, the story of the Eighth Air Force is virtually unknown. They can tell you about the battle of Gettysburg or the battle for Baghdad, and perhaps the drama associated with Pearl Harbor, thanks to the efforts of the movie and television industries, but they know little if anything about the most spectacular bombing campaign the world has ever witnessed. Writers of current texts have largely scaled back on the coverage of the military aspects of World War II, and consequently, with the exception of the dropping of the A-bomb on Hiroshima, give scant attention, if any, to the air war. Veterans of the Eighth Air Force, as members of the Eighth Air Force Historical Society, attempt to fill this dearth of knowledge through speaking engagements whenever and wherever they can find an audience. While their personal stories are somewhat restricted to a relatively brief period on the air war when they were completing their required twenty-five to thirty-five missions, their accounts thrill their listeners, especially young people, who never realized such heroics were part of recent history and would like to know more.

That responsibility has been taken on by military historians who have filled library shelves with many accounts of the air war from many different perspectives. While I cover very little history of the air war that is new in the pages that follow, and I don't reinterpret the controversial aspects of strategic bombardment, I will attempt to span the history of the Mighty Eighth from its origin to the end of the war through a mixture of key historical events and autobiographical sketches derived from oral and written testimonies. This includes coverage of the home front the airmen left behind, their training and experiences that led to assignment to bomber bases in England, their daily encounters with the British, the experiences of airmen who had the misfortune to become prisoners of war, and finally, the return of the veterans to the life they left behind when they went off to war.

The remarkable development of the Eighth Air Force as it grew from little more than a concept in 1941 to the powerful war machine it became in 1945 dumfounded even the most confident air enthusiasts. How the leaders took the thousands of B-17 Flying Fortresses and Liberators with their fighter escorts, and carried out "daylight precision bombing" on every conceivable target of Hitler's Fortress Europe, is in itself a remarkable story. However, this magnificent effort was not accomplished without controversy. As early as 1942, American commanders were embroiled in debate with their British counterparts regarding the advisability of conducting daylight precision bombing operations vis-a-vis Royal Air Force Bomber Command's approach of night time "area bombing." Neither country would give in on its particular strategy, and in the last year of the war the line between the two concepts was often blurred as both air forces were charged with being guilty of "terror bombing" of German civilians, a precursor to a tactic later used against Japan. Air enthusiasts and historians over the past decades have relied primarily on the *United States Strategic Bombing Survey* published in 1949 and various accounts from Royal Air Force Bomber Command Commander, Sir Arthur Harris, and American commanders of the air war, to evaluate both the American strategy and results of the total bombing efforts. In 1995, fifty years after the end of the war, Harris's *Dispatch on War Operations* provided insight into the official British role in Strategic bombing. It was followed in 1998 by *The Official*

Report of the British Bombing Survey, the long-awaited British version of the *United States Bombing Survey,* that was first published in 1947. Hundreds of other biographies, autobiographies, and histories of the air war have been written and enhanced by the story of the Eighth as exhibited in museums both in the United States and in the United Kingdom. Most recently, scholarship on the subject has been helped by the opening of the records depositories at the Eighth Air Force Museum in Savannah, Georgia. Finally, the Air Force History Office files at the Air University, Maxwell Air Force Base Montgomery, continues to be the primary source for records of all Eighth Air Force organizations including official histories of all bomb groups. The controversy may never completely be resolved, but recent scholarship certainly facilitates analysis of the events.

Prior to March of 1943, Eighth Air Force officials devoted time and limited resources to a trial-and-error period of learning how to conduct strategic bombing missions. Faced with an insufficient number of aircraft and crews, American commanders had to get their feet on the ground while attempting to prove to their British counterparts that they could do the job. By mid-1943, the first formation of American bombers began operations deep into Germany, unfortunately without fighter escorts, all the way to the target. Due to heavy losses such missions had to be discontinued for the winter months raising serious doubts as to the future of daylight precision bombing.

At the same time missions were directed at preparation for the long-awaited second front to follow with the invasion of Normandy in June of that year. Following D-day, oil became the major target, and together with transportation and other tactical targets in support of ground operations consumed most bombing efforts until the final Eighth Air Force mission on April 25, 1945. Avoiding a mission-by-mission discussion of each phase, a near impossible task considering the fact that the Mighty Eighth bombed enemy targets 459 days in the course of the European War, often hitting several targets on a single day, I have selected those that seem to best represent the turning points of the air war and integrating personal accounts with the history.

In addition to accounts of bombing missions, the story would not be complete without a discussion of the men who saw their flying time in bombers cut short when they became prisoners of war. While the POW story is not unique to the Air Force, airmen of the Mighty Eighth were major occupants of the German Stalags, especially Stalag Luft I and III, and their experiences provide the reader with clear evidence of the personal price they paid undergoing such an ordeal. I have chosen six personal accounts that illustrate to a remarkable degree what those men went through. In many ways they are representative of myriad POWs who went from evasion, to capture, to prison life, through the infamous "long march" in the frigid winter of 1945, to eventual release.

I close this book where it began, with the men who were the backbone of the Eighth Air Force, and their return to the homes they left behind. The "Alabama bomber boys" had gone full circle from the somewhat idyllic world of 1941 to the post war in which they attempted to pick up where they left off. Many returned to families they hardly knew, that had fought their own war of rationing and sacrifice, while not knowing where their loved ones were, much less the horrific ordeals they were experiencing. Some stayed in the Air Force, while others picked up the pieces of their lives and settled down in occupations they left behind. Others took advantage of the most lucrative veterans' benefits in history and went to college. Of course, as so many veterans of World War II will attest, life after the horrors in the sky over Europe was never the same. Memories, some good and many bad, would haunt them the rest of their lives. No efforts at return to normalcy could erase the nightmares acquired on those deadly missions. Boys had become men, and though damaged irreparably with their own ghosts, they do not hesitate to proclaim that they are much better men because of what they went through, and as such enriched their communities in ways they never dreamed on that Sunday afternoon in 1941.

1

December 7, 1941: Lives at the Crossroads

Today all of us are in the same boat with you and the people of the Empire, and it is a ship which must not and cannot be sunk
            Roosevelt to Churchill
            December 8, 1941

The nation was in its last hours of peace—a typical Sunday morning with no hint that before the sun set, the events of December 7, 1941, would usher in not only the worst war it had ever experienced, but also major changes in the lives of its citizens. An Asian country both distant from its shores, and unfamiliar with its culture, was about to strike not only the American fleet at Pearl Harbor, but also at the heartstrings of countless Americans.

Even after six decades most Americans who were above the age of eight remember that day and the moment they heard the news of the attack. They remember where they were, to whom they were talking, and what they were doing. So it was with the nation's youth, many still in high school, or having recently graduated, or taking their place in the work force. In the days that followed, many of their lives took a new direction as they answered their nation's call to serve, some on the home front, but many in the armed forces. Among the latter, thousands of young men would elect to serve in the newest military service, the Army Air Forces, and 350,000 of that number would eventually become members of the Eighth Air Force, an organization that did not even exist on that day. They were soon to go to war in the deadly skies over Europe, and as such, their lives and those of their girl friends, wives, and families, would change in profound and dramatic ways.

In every town and city across America, the pattern was the same—a quiet Sunday, suddenly transformed in a matter of moments. Collectively, America's future warriors were in their late teens or no more than a year or so past their twentieth birthday. Their worlds, for the most part, were confined to less than a hundred-mile radius of their homes. They had come out of the depression, watched their fathers struggle for survival, and were beginning to share the American dream, that appeared to offer them decent employment, a wife and family, and in most instances a home tied to local roots.

On the previous day many had enjoyed the festivities of the opening of the Christmas season. Birmingham, Alabama, was typical of cities and towns across America, as shoppers flooded the sidewalks, many disembarking from crowded streetcars that clanged their way through the city's downtown area. The *Montgomery Advertiser* reported a similar scene in the central shopping district of the capital city. Its front page headline read, "Store Windows Shine Again in Yuletide Array." Like Birmingham, the city had lifted a ban on outdoor lighting, bringing "jubilation," and the paper reported that with the approach of dusk, "the city's brilliance after weeks of gloom was startling."[1]

As Americans settled down for Sunday lunch and prepared for a quiet and restful afternoon, an ocean and a half away, 351 Japanese aircraft, commanded by Mitsuo Fuchida, headed for Oahu in the Hawaiian Islands, homing in on radio signals emitted from Honolulu radio stations. At 7:53, the torpedo planes, fighters and bombers struck the unsuspecting Pacific Fleet, and in the next hour and fifty-seven minutes crippled the American navy and air force in a near perfectly coordinated attack throughout the island.

Meanwhile, across the air waves, radio stations were broadcasting an array of music, Sunday sermons, and football. At 1:25 p.m., in the game between the New York Giants and the Brooklyn Dodgers, Ward Cliff had just returned a Brooklyn kick-off to his twenty-seven yard line, when station WOR in New York broke in with the news that Pearl Harbor had been bombed. After a brief pause the game resumed.

Audiences attending theaters and sporting events, and patrons of other activities, heard the news over the next two hours, while many other Americans were stunned out of their Sunday slumber by the interruption of their radio programs. At Cloverdale Junior High School, in Montgomery Alabama, Wesley Newton was watching a football game between two high schools. The driver of a pickup truck that had been used to transport equipment heard the announcement over the radio. When he told some players, one asked, "Where's Pearl Harbor?" Another asked: "who bombed?"[2] Diana Polen, of Huntsville, Alabama, was twelve years old, but remembers that she was "midway on the staircase of her home. "My dad was sitting in the club chair below," she said, and "we looked at each other shocked from the news on our radio."[3] Raymond Hill of Gadsden, Alabama, was with friends at a movie theater. "When we got out onto the sidewalk," he remembers, "we were stunned by the news and by the realization that we would all most surely be called into the service."[4] Frank Bolen, of Selma, Alabama, was at Montevallo College to pick up his date, Frances. His one recollection, like so many Americans that day was, "disbelief."[5]

Henry Arnold, a senior in Alexander City High School, thought the news was a joke. That reaction must have come to mind two years later as he looked down from his B-17 ball turret gun position thirty thousand feet over Berlin at a carpet of antiaircraft flak tearing holes in his bomber formation. Henry's future wife, Amy Barbaree, a student at Sydney Lanier High School in Montgomery, believed the attack to be impossible. A couple of days earlier she had read about Pearl Harbor in the *Current Events Newsletter,* and about how well it was defended.[6]

How does one grasp the enormity of such an event? The answers varied, and while virtually everyone can remember the moment they heard the news, memories related to the remainder of that Sunday and the days that followed were clouded at best. Dora Hill, from Gadsden, Alabama, wife to be of Raymond Hill, experienced the typical day in the average American household, remembering that "We spent the rest of the day and the evening listening to reports of the reaction from all over the United States, and by shortwave, the reaction from around the world."[7] But for Joy O' Rourke of Mobile, Alabama, memories were more emotional though brief and to the point: "I cried when I heard the news," she said. Her only other thought was of the "many young men who might be killed," and especially for her high school sweetheart, Owen O'Rourke, who would surely be called into the service.[8]

But for many citizens the events of that day created many questions and a great deal of confusion. What would happen next? Would the enemy invade American shores? Could the country expect to be bombed? Would the United States declare war on Germany as well as Japan? How many men would be needed to defeat the enemy? Would it be a long war or a short one? And for the more pessimistic, could their nation lose?

On December 8, Americans were greeted by a variety of news coverage of the attack that was sketchy at best or entirely inaccurate at worst. Most Americans were at the mercy of conflicting radio or newspaper reports, and therefore had many questions as to the extent of the damage inflicted on the Pacific base. For example, the *Montgomery Advertiser* greeted its readers with the headline, JAPS KILL 350 AMERICANS IN SURPRISE ATTACK, a number to be raised to approximately ninety in the days to come. But that figure was not surprising when the *Honolulu Star-Bulletin* reported in its second extra edition on December 7, "over 400 deaths," and on the eighth reported that saboteurs had landed in the islands.[9] While there was much confusion in the minds of Americans for several days to come, President Roosevelt put many doubts to rest concerning the future when he asked Congress to declare war on Japan, a declaration that was quickly followed by reciprocal declarations of war on the United States by the other two Axis powers, Germany and Italy. Schools throughout the country held special convocations for students to hear the President, and in many instances conducted special prayers for the nation and its leaders. When Roosevelt delivered one of his famous "fireside chats" the Birmingham Symphony Orchestra interrupted its performance for a half hour to permit the audience to hear his comments.[10]

The young men who later took to the skies as part of the Eighth Air Force collectively remember that their one concern from the time they heard the news was not "if" they would go into service, but "which service" and "when." Dr. George H, Denny, President of The University of Alabama, tried to soothe the fears of students by reminding them that "selective service" did not mean "elective service." He encouraged students to "take the long view and stick by their academic guns."[11] Evidently, he, like many other Alabamians, did not grasp the reality that the nation was in for a long ordeal and that every able-bodied man would be needed. Certainly, no one expected an eventual fighting force of some sixteen million men to be drawn from university and college ranks across the nation as well as every other walk of life as the needs of the military dictated. Students facing graduation from high school suddenly put aside all plans for future education or employment, while some, like seventeen year old Lawson Corley, were upset that they were still in high school and too young to enlist immediately.[12]

Newspapers throughout the remainder of the month reported the doubts, fears, and uncertainty that prevailed across the nation. As early as the Monday following the attack, *The Birmingham News* reported the mobilization of G-men within the state to guard against sabotage, especially around munitions factories. Specific G-men activities were censored. The same edition reported an FBI investigation of a dinner held in late November attended by fifteen Japanese. The article read that they came in two's or three's "to avoid suspicion." It did not reveal the reason for the suspicion. That incident was related to the mistrust of Japanese citizens and non-citizens across the country that never subsided for the duration of the war, and in places, especially on the west coast, would lead to sad injustices. *The Birmingham* News indicated that about 30 Japanese lived in the state, with six in Birmingham. Several Japanese truck farmers in the Mobile area were put under "close surveillance."[13]

On December 8, a Presbyterian minister who was living in "Trinity Negro School" in Limestone County was one of seven suspicious aliens arrested along with five Germans and one Italian. He worked for the American Missionary Association. On December 9, the FBI advised anyone with a complaint about an alien to call the FBI office and not to try to take action on their own. In a clear illustration of the extent of hatred for the Japanese, newspapers on December 25, reported on the destruction of Japanese Cherry trees in Washington, D.C. Four of the largest trees had been cut down and the zealots who did the deed had written, "To hell with those Japanese" on severed tree trunks.[14]

Many Americans, especially in large cities in the Western and Eastern United States feared attacks by the enemy. On December 23, defense officials in Washington warned cities within 300 miles of the oceans that they were in danger, should the nation be attacked.[15] Consequently such cities began immediately to establish civil defense programs. Meanwhile, across the nation, state military units became part of the general mobilization efforts. In no place was this better illustrated than at the recruiting stations. On December 9, The *Montgomery Advertiser* reported "Recruiting Stations Thronged by Young Alabamians" and went on to state the obvious, that "Japan's dastardly attack on Hawaii had the blood of many Alabamians boiling." For the many men already in uniform at various military installations in Alabama, such as Maxwell Field in Montgomery, December 8 brought immediate alert status. That Army Air Forces base with its large cadre of high ranking officers and training facilities, was one of thirty in the Southeast alerted to possible sabotage activities, along with Brookley Field in Mobile, Gunter Field, also in Montgomery, and Craig Air Corps training base in Selma.[16] With so many air fields, Alabamians had much exposure to the presence of military aviation, and many of the young men who were eager to enlist in the Army Air Forces were already flying enthusiasts in 1941.

In spite of the events of December 7, young men destined to soon wear the uniform and their families celebrated Christmas much as they had in the past. Rationing was a few weeks away and the day was resplendent with all of the decorations and spirit of past Christmases. Even the newspapers addressed the holiday spirit in their Christmas editions. However, in spite of efforts to forget what was happening elsewhere, behind the celebrations were the ominous feelings that could not be dismissed. In

Alabama, the *Fayette County Times* paralleled an article on Christmas services with the sad news that the surprise attack on December 7 had left three Alabamians from Fayette County, Alabama unaccounted for. Pleas for volunteers to serve both in the military and in civil defense became standard reading in papers across the nation.[17] In Birmingham, the call went out over the air waves on the afternoon of the attack causing scores of young men to flood the recruiting offices when they opened on Monday.[18] On December 24, the recruiting offices in Montgomery announced that they would be open on Christmas.[19]

And there was no shortage of interest from men of all ages to serve their country in any way possible. At Starke University School in Montgomery, students were too young to enlist. However when the *Advertiser* referred to the attack as "Japan's knife-in-the-back attack on U.S. possessions," students were so infuriated that "they all went down and volunteered for civilian defense work, 100 percent strong."[20] H.B. Ledbetter of Gunter's Mountain, Alabama, was 74, and was turned down for service, but promised he would get out his squirrel gun and "fill any Japs full of lead if they came his way."[21]

Even the attempts of sports-minded readers to escape from the events of the world through reading accounts of sporting events was not always successful. As Alabama prepared to play Texas A&M in the Cotton Bowl, a game it won, the *Birmingham News* editor reminded sports enthusiasts that for many of the players, it would not only be their last game, but some who would join Uncle Sam would play in "one game that must be won against the foulest combination of cut throats the world has ever known."[22]

As the last remnants of turkey, cranberry sauce, and pumpkin pie were consumed, and the Bowl games were history, a process that was already underway across America consumed the interest and actions of thousands of its young men. They pondered many serious questions. What service would they enter? Should they wait for the draft? Should they leave college or seek deferment at least through the remainder of the school year? Should they try to leave high school before graduation and join the Navy, the one service that would take them at age seventeen? Answers to the questions varied, but for the most part, and certainly among the subjects of this study, one thing was certain—they wanted to do their part, and the sooner the better. For hundreds of those young men, their search ended in an organization still in its embryo stage in the opening days of the war; an organization destined for glory. They would be part of what would eventually be called the "mighty" Eighth Air Force. They entered the Eighth's ranks because they wanted to fly, having no concept about what that desire meant in 1942.

The Eighth Air Force was the outgrowth of an enormous expansion of the Army Air Forces that had been in the planning stages long before December 7. Even so, when war came, the entire Army Air Forces only had an authorized strength of 348,535 officers and men. On December 23, 1941, the Air Staff agreed on the first of several plans to bring in fifty thousand new pilots annually along with three hundred thousand technicians. On January 3, 1942, President Roosevelt directed an aircraft production goal of one hundred thirty-one thousand by December 1945, or a total of ten thousand aircraft a month.[23] The air war was front and center, and few military strategists realized just how massive the future air armada was to be. Among those, were a group of officers at Savannah, Georgia, who on January 28, 1942, activated the Eighth Air Force. General Hap Arnold, Chief of Staff of the Army Air Force, appointed Colonel Asa N. Duncan, soon to be Brigadier General, of Leighton, Alabama, to be the commander of the task force that would organize the fledgling organization.

Meanwhile, the enlistment and induction programs were in full gear, and churning out the men who would enter Army, Navy, Marines, and other military services to form the largest and most efficient fighting machine in American military history. While that process varied according to the type of service involved, the desires of the participants, and most significantly the needs of the military, the men experienced some of the same uncertainties, frustrations, homesickness, confusion and a whole lot of "hurry up and wait" before finding their niche in the rapid expanding military. Those with aspirations to fly generally had to be twenty-one to be a pilot, unless they could obtain a waiver with their parents' approval. All other positions required that the applicant be at least eighteen. The process always began at the recruiting station or the induction station, and each volunteer or draftee had a different experience depending on local station quotas.

Charles Shinault, had experiences that were typical of the eager men who wanted to fly. He enlisted at Camp Shelby, Mississippi, in 1943. From there he went to Maxwell Air Force Base, Alabama, for pre-flight; to Avon Park, Florida, for primary; to Cochran Field, Georgia, for basic flight training; and finally Blytheville, Arkansas, for advanced twin engine instruction. After that, he was assigned to a B-17 crew for training and preparation for overseas. Each step along the way from Camp Shelby to Blytheville was filled with uncertainty—physical problems, failed check rides, accidents, changing needs of the service, etc., and any one of many things could cause a would-be pilot to wash out of flying training.[24]

Shinault's experiences varied from other individuals, especially those who were destined for gunnery or engineer training. Men too young for enlistment or still in high school, such as William O. Holcomb of Birmingham, were permitted to enlist in the Enlisted Reserve Corps to await eligibility for the aviation cadet program. Upon graduation they immediately volunteered for induction. Holcombe reported to Keesler Field, Biloxi, Mississippi, and after processing and the inevitable "hurry up and wait" routine, was sent to Texas Tech to prepare for the aviation cadet program. Unfortunately, while in school, he was told that the Air Force had six thousand too many applicants for flight training. He then volunteered and was accepted for flight engineer training. In his experiences with travel out of the South, he traveled first to Santa Anna, California, and then to Amarillo, Texas, followed by aerial gunnery school in Las Vegas. Once training was complete, Holcomb was assigned to McDill Air Force Base, Florida, where he joined a B-17 crew as a flight engineer and gunner, destined for the newest Armed Service, the Eighth Air Force.[25]

Raymond Hill represented a second category of inductees and entered the Army by way of the draft. He was unsure as to what branch of the army he would enter until just before he was to be shipped overseas, when the Army asked for volunteers for aerial gunnery duty. He volunteered and entered gunnery training at Buckingham Army Air Field, Fort Myers, Florida.[26] Louis Kline, who grew up in the depressed area of Western Pennsylvania, represented still another scenario. Two months before the war, at the age of 16, he forged his father's name and entered the Army

Air Corps (as the Air Force was designated prior to 1941). He then followed the usual pattern from basic to airplane mechanics school to crew assignment to shipment overseas. Kline's early assignment to a B-17 crew would take him to Europe in 1943 and put him in the deadliest part of the air war just as he turned eighteen.[27]

Glenn Taylor did not set out to fly. In fact, as he left his freshman class at North Carolina State College to enlist, he did so for one reason, and that was to serve the Army wherever needed. His exam results were such as to place him in aircraft maintenance engineering school at Keesler Air Field, Biloxi Mississippi. Since each engineer also had to do double duty as a bomber crew gunner, he then entered gunnery school followed by crew assignment in a B-17.[28]

Exact assignment to meet the Air Force needs was always iffy at best, and as has always been true, "the needs of the service" took priority while physical status and flying aptitude often determined the final position the enlistee would occupy in the Mighty Eighth. John Hard took an interesting route to eventually become a B-17 pilot and is representative of the dichotomy of the process from enlistment desires to actual assignment. He was first turned down for the aviation cadet program due to what the doctor referred to as "an eye accommodation" problem. But, determined to fly, he underwent an eye exercise program to pass his test. In the meantime, he changed his mind and attempted to join the Navy Air Corps, where he saw a better opportunity to become a fighter pilot. When he completed his application and truthfully reported that he had previously been turned down by the Army, he was informed, that "the Navy never accepts anybody turned down by the Army." So, he went back to the Army, and that time he passed the tests, and became a pilot. Then, the "needs of the service" cranked in, and he did not get to fly fighters, as he had hoped, but instead became a
B-17 pilot.[29]

Like many other recruits who entered the Army Air Forces, Hard knew little about what was ahead of him. Instead of the glamour that was so much a part of the mystique of becoming a fighter pilot, he soon became a member of a ten-man bomber crew destined to fly at twenty-five thousand or more feet in a non-pressurized and unheated bomber in a life and death struggle against the best pilots the German Luftwaffe had to offer. Just one trip in a B-17 Flying Fortress, a B-24 Liberator, or one of the fighter aircraft assigned to escort the huge bombers, provided more excitement than many Americans would endure in a life time; situations where lives hung in the balance, and survival was often in doubt. However, Hard was willing to serve where he was needed, and would eventually complete thirty-five grueling missions.[30]

Lawson Corley was a native of the small town of Docent, Alabama, a mere dot on the map, unknown even to many people in his own state. He grew up in the hardest of times. His father, a plant manager for a steel mill, was killed in a car wreck in 1934 that crippled his mother and injured him. Over the next six years Lawson's fatherless family of his mother and four brothers struggled to survive the depression. In 1937, the family moved to the Woodlawn area of Birmingham where he graduated from high school in 1942, six months after the beginning of the war.

Corley was not happy about waiting to graduate before enlisting, and even tried to enlist the day after Pearl Harbor, but was told he had to be eighteen. He had always been fascinated by airplanes although he had never flown. So, when he reached the magic age, he applied for pilot training, took all of the tests and happily was accepted. In early 1943 he entered pre-flight training at Maxwell Air Force Base followed by primary training at Turner Air Force Base, Albany, Georgia. There, he found himself in trouble after buzzing a church on one of his flights. He washed out of flight training, but was permitted to go to bombardier school. He graduated and received his bombardier wings and commission on September 13, 1943. Following three days of leave, he reported to Mitchel Field, New York, where he joined the B-24 crew that would be his family in the months to come. Awaiting him was a near death situation and the horror of a German prison camp.[31]

Like Corley, Roy Davidson, William Lawley, Jr., and Bill Massey were representative of the men who dreamed of flying, and jumped at the first opportunity to enlist, rather than wait for induction. Davidson, one year ahead of Corley in Woodlawn High School in Birmingham, had always been fascinated with airplanes and, prior to December 7, had begun studying to pass the pilot entrance exam. Prior to 1942, a pilot candidate had to be twenty years old and have completed two years of college for acceptance in the program. A candidate not meeting the school requirement could apply for a waiver, and if he passed, enter the program. In January 1942 when the age requirement dropped to eighteen, Davidson immediately volunteered and was sent to Montgomery for testing. He passed all physical and mental tests and in March was called up for flight training at Maxwell Field. From there he followed the normal sequence from primary training to basic training and finally twin engine advanced training at Columbus, Mississippi. Due to high scores that placed him first in his training element of four trainees, he had his choice as to his future. He requested immediate assignment to B-17s, because "that was the quickest way to get into action and win the war." He got his wish, and within a year would endure death defying experiences that went far beyond anything he could have imagined back at Columbus, Mississippi.[32]

Shortly after Davidson entered primary flight training, Lawley left his service station job in Birmingham, and reported for aviation training at Maxwell Air Force Base. Like Davidson, he knew he wanted to fly, and began an almost identical process to the one experienced by Davidson, receiving his wings and Second Lieutenant commission in April 1943. He had no idea that the year to follow would place him in the ranks of the select few survivors to receive the Medal of Honor.[33]

Bill Massey became very familiar with the fact that miracles do happen. He too wanted to go to war as soon as possible, and like Corley, Davidson, and Lawley, looked to the excitement of flying. And, like the others, he had never been in an airplane. Massey received his wings and commission in June of 1943, and was assigned to Lockbourne Air Force Base, Ohio, where he trained to fly B-17s. His escape from death would come over Germany, when he was blown out of a B-17—without a parachute.[34]

Thousands of other young men from California to Rhode Island, and Minnesota to Mississippi, had experiences similar to those of Corley, Davidson, Lawley, and Massey, and became proud members of the Eighth Air Force. On December 7, 1941, they were "boys" who knew nothing beyond the confines of their home and community, and they certainly knew nothing about the huge Air Force they were about to enter. But enter they did—and proudly. They became part of the magnificent heritage of air power, and in so doing created many of the legends that gave the Eighth its proud title of "The Mighty Eighth."

2

What Was the Eighth Air Force?

But the advent of air power that can go directly to the vital centers and entirely neutralize or destroy them has put a completely new complexion on the old system of war....

Billy Mitchell

Glenn Taylor was a pre-aeronautical engineering student at North Carolina State College when a classmate interrupted his studying in the library with the startling announcement that "The Japs have just bombed Pearl Harbor." We all knew what that meant," he said, "but had no idea which direction fate would take us." He was soon to find out, and for the next three years, the war that so suddenly broke the quiet on his college campus became an integral part of his life. Indeed, college life was put on hold, indefinitely. Two and a half years later, on April 7, 1944, following a process that took him from induction into the Army Air Forces, to completion of aviation engineering and gunnery schools, Taylor received orders assigning him as a B-24 gunner in the Eighth Air Force. Like many others who preceded him, he had little concept of the magnitude of that organization's mission, nor the reality of the war he was about to enter.[1]

Taylor's uncertainty changed to concern when he was advised upon his arrival at the 466th Bomb Group, Atterbridge Air Base, England, that he "might as well consider himself dead as statistics were weighed against...survival." By the time he completed his required twenty-five combat missions in October 1944, he had beaten those odds and went on to complete thirty-two missions, and like so many other Eighth Air Force airmen, he had learned to appreciate his small albeit critical role in helping to fulfill the dreams that air power advocates, so-called air power prophets, had advocated over the previous three decades.[2]

Colonel (later Brigadier General) Asa N. Duncan, from Leighton, Alabama, played an even larger role in the fledgling organization when Lieutenant General Henry (Hap) Arnold, Chief of the Army Air Forces, appointed him as Eighth Air Force Chief of Staff. As one of the old breed of officers involved in the struggle for air power between the wars, he had dreamed of the day when the airplane, especially the bomber, could live up to its potential. Like Generals Arnold, Carl (Tooey) Spaatz, Ira Eaker, and Jimmy Doolittle, all names associated with the Air Force's struggle for respectability, his service dated back to World War I, when he left the infantry to participate in what was at that time called the Army Air Service. He was decorated for "exceptional coolness and bravery" during the final Allied offensive on the Western Front, and his continuous service from 1918 to 1942 prepped him to play a critical role in the establishment of the Eighth Air Force.

Unfortunately, Duncan's life was one of the many "what might have been" stories of World War II. On November 17, 1942, while in route to England from North Africa, his aircraft caught fire for an unknown reason and crashed into the sea 136 miles off the English coast. In spite of a massive air-sea rescue effort, neither the aircraft nor crew were found, thus ending the life of one of the early aviation pioneers and the first of five Eighth Air Force commanders. He was also the second American general to be killed in the war. In the citation to accompany his Distinguished Service Medal, awarded posthumously, General Spaatz recognized Duncan's service and credited him with playing a critical role in the war effort during the uncertain early months of 1942.³

While Duncan's life was cut short, his legacy and that of the many air power theorists began to come to fruition the month he died. On November 1, 1942, the Eighth Air Force flew its first bombing mission against the rail marshaling yards at Rouen-Sotteville, France. From then until it dropped its last bomb on the ball bearing factory at Pilsen, Czechoslovakia, April 25, 1945, the Eighth flew 330,523 total sorties and dropped 686,406 tons of bombs on Hitler's "Fortress Europe," a significant accomplishment for an organization that did not exist when the war began.

Step by step the concept of strategic bombardment, long the dream of the air enthusiasts who preceded Duncan and his cohorts, was matched with the means to make it a reality. The efforts were to be painful and at times seemed impossible to men such as Taylor and some two hundred ten thousand other airmen who flew combat missions with the Eighth during the three years it was engaged in the air war. Sadly, twenty-six thousand of their number paid the supreme price in the effort, while twenty-eight thousand became prisoners of war.

The concept behind long range strategic bombing and the aircraft to carry it out dated back to World War I. Prior to American involvement, the Germans, French, and British sporadically bombed their opponent's targets with limited success. By the end of the war all of those nations had traded some significant blows from the air against their enemy's capitals. In 1915, Germany even engaged in Zeppelin attacks on English cities, in what would later be referred to as terror bombing. By 1918, America and her allies took bombing to a new level with large-scale air tactical support of the final offensives of the war. In the largest of these efforts, Brigadier General William (Billy) Mitchell successfully directed some fourteen hundred aircraft in support of the allied Meuse-Argonne offensive. The airplane, while still in its infancy for effective use as a bomber, had proven its worth at least in the minds of air enthusiasts.

Mitchell carried over his war-time experiences into the inter-war years, thereby becoming America's most outspoken advocate of the role of air power in future wars. In league with such air power prophets as General Guilio Douhet, Italian exponent of using strategic bombing to win a war, and Royal Air Force Major General Sir Hugh Trenchard and his advocacy of an independent air force, Mitchell joined a vocal minority within the War Department in attempting to convince hardened generals that the airplane had a place in future military operations, not only for support of ground operations, but as an independent instrument for strategic bombing.

By 1925, Mitchell's controversial views on the possibilities of the airplane as a strategic bomber and his outspoken criticism of the Army and Navy brass, who continued to see the airplane as just an extension of artillery, so angered his superiors that he was court-martialed. In a much publicized trial he was found guilty of insubordination and forced to resign. Mitchell's views however, in writing and in speeches, continued to incite interest and some anger in and out of the War and Navy Departments throughout the inter-war years. In 1925, he expressed some of his most significant concepts in his book, *Winged Defense,* where he wrote that in a future war aircraft could be expected to strike directly at the enemy's "centers of production of all kinds, means of transportation, agricultural areas, [and] ports and shipping....They will destroy the means of making war."[4] Translated and interpreted seventeen years later by Eighth Air Force commanders, those views, in effect defined "daylight precision bombing."

Meanwhile, air power prophets from Great Britain, the United States, and other countries continued the debate with army and navy leaders over the significant role of air power, especially bombers, in any future war. Like Mitchell, many of those veterans had witnessed the carnage on the battlefields of the "great war" and were convinced that technology had rendered the techniques of that conflict obsolete and that future wars would be won from the air. They envisioned huge fleets of bombers hitting cities and strategic targets or "vital centers" in the opening days of a conflict, and bringing such chaos to the enemy that victory could come swiftly and without the slaughter of massive armies. They saw the long bitter struggles vis-a-vis the World War I battlefields as no longer relevant.

For successful implementation of their concepts, the prophets also engaged in other serious debates. Led by Trenchard, and encouraged by Mitchell, they vigorously appealed for an independent air force in which military aviation of the future would be separate from the age old exclusive supporting roles of their respective armies and navies. Trenchard was more successful than the American airmen and persuaded his British cohorts that the airplane was about to revolutionize warfare. Therefore, after much debate, British military brass and Government officials agreed to create a separate air arm, thereby achieving autonomy for the British air force. Their first hand experience in World War I with German attacks on Britain, in which 857 British citizens were killed in fifty-two air raids, added credibility to his arguments and influenced the decision. Along with the perceived strategic bombing concept that could take the war to the enemy's homeland, British military leaders also remembered the critical role tactical air power played in breaking the stalemate during the final offensives on the Western front. Therefore, in March of 1918, the British army and navy air forces were combined into the Royal Air Force, a third and co-equal branch of the British armed forces. Air power had achieved its first victory in the battle for an autonomous service that could demonstrate the potential of the airplane.

In spite of such success in Britain, the pleas of Mitchell, Spaatz, Eaker and other American airmen fell on the deaf ears of an American public and Congress tied to isolation and budgetary restraints. The long road toward such independence gained its first semblance of respect when Congress passed the Air Corps Act of 1926, and changed the Air Service as it was then called to the Army Air Corps, thereby placing it under the Army General Staff. But its mission continued to be confined to supporting ground forces, and would continue to be so until the passage of the National Defense Act of 1947.

From the mid-nineteen thirties until the opening of the war in Europe, the air theorists debated both among themselves, and especially with the army and navy brass, the role of the bomber in future conflicts. Much Air Corps debate took place at the Air Corps Tactical School (ACTS), a think tank located at Maxwell Field, Montgomery, Alabama. While the ACTS had the responsibility of providing professional training for the officers who would lead the fledgling Air Corps, it also was assigned the task of developing air doctrine. There, the airmen debated the totality of air power as they then envisioned it. While to many that meant strategy tied to so called "pursuit aviation" and the use of fighter aircraft, many others were advocates of "high altitude bombardment" and selective bombing especially aimed at vital centers within the country of a future adversary.[5] While the school went on to stress targets related to military forces and the economic substructure of a nation, the term "vital centers" was to be open to interpretation and the cause of much discussion and many arguments in the war that followed.

Of course, all of the above would have been irrelevant without a bomber with sufficient range, bomb load, and accuracy to carry out those objectives. Recognizing how crucial the technical side of air power was, the theorists at the school devoted much of their time attempting to match target selection to the means of bomb delivery. Some of their enthusiasm and incessant requests finally caught the attention of officials within the War Department, and by 1935 Congress appropriated sufficient funds for production of a prototype of a bomber to carry out future strategic objectives. Therefore, in July, the Boeing aircraft company under contract with the Army, introduced the experimental XB-17 long range bomber to Air Corps procurement officials. By the end of that year, in spite of some technical difficulties that included crashing the first test model, the War Department not only accepted the bomber, then named the Flying Fortress, but ordered thirteen of the huge aircraft to be built as the beginning of a long-range strategic bomber fleet, the first of 12,371 to be built over the next ten years.

The Flying Fortress was unique from any aircraft ever produced. It was seventy-four feet, and nine inches in length with a wing span of 103 feet nine inches. Its maximum speed was 287 mph and its operating range was 1,100 miles. It could reach a ceiling of thirty-five thousand feet with a maximum bomb load of 12,800 pounds. It was armed with ten fifty-caliber machine guns mounted in the nose, ball (underneath), waists and tail positions, thus providing coverage against attacking aircraft from any direction. On occasion the "F" and "G" models, the last to be built, could house an additional three fifty-caliber guns. When involved in the air war over Germany, the Flying Fortress proved to be remarkably resilient and able to withstand an enormous amount of punishment and damage. It was exactly the type of bomber the air theorists had in mind as they worked on contingency plans in the prewar years.

Two years after the B-17 entered the inventory, Consolidated Aircraft Company introduced its contribution to the heavy bomber fleet, the XB-24. Following successful testing in 1941, the first B-24 Liberators rolled off the assembly line. The Royal Air Force, then conducting bombing missions deep into Germany, added the Liberators to its long range bomber fleet. In November 1941, the Army Air Forces took delivery of the huge bombers. The B-24 had a seven-foot longer wing span and a seven-foot shorter fuselage. One of its major attributes was its range which was double the capacity of the B-17. While its speed of 290 mph was similar to the B-17, it was somewhat limited to a ceiling of twenty-eight thousand feet and carried a four-thousand-pound less bomb load. Due to its range capability, the Liberator was the only bomber capable of patrolling the vast reaches of the Pacific or Atlantic oceans. Its versatility also enabled it to double as a cargo plane in the China-Burma theater where it was designated the C-87. With some modification the B-24 was also used by the Navy, where it was designated the PB4y Privateer. But like the B-17, the Liberator played a crucial role in long range bombing missions, thereby creating a potent double punch against the Axis. By the conclusion of the war 18,190 of the huge bombers had been built.

While the two heavy bombers fulfilled the dreams of the air prophets and the desires of Air Force leaders attempting to turn dreams into reality, they were not invincible weapon systems. The men who took them to war found shortcomings that proved very costly, especially on long-range missions that became so much a part of Eighth Air Force operations. The bombers were designed not only to fly such distances to the very heart of Nazi Germany, but also to defend themselves against the enemy fighters trying to knock them out of the sky, while subjected to the deadly antiaircraft fire from the ground known as flak. And, as if a determined enemy was not enough to make American air crews miserable, they also had to contend with no heat in sixty-degrees-below-zero weather while at the mercy of uncomfortable and not always dependable oxygen masks, so critical at such high altitudes.

The bombers were designed around the concept that in tight formations with machine guns firing in all directions they could destroy or drive off enemy fighters, even without fighter escorts. So the concept went. In reality, men of the Eighth Air Force discovered, especially in the dark days of 1943, that the Luftwaffe's Messerschmitt Me-109s and Focke Wulf Fw-190s, could penetrate even the tightest formations and consequently take a terrible toll on both aircraft and crews. While the enemy suffered innumerable losses in knocking holes in the American formations, that was little solace to the men who watched their formations decimated by the determined and experienced Luftwaffe pilots.

The air power theorists in the Air Corps Tactical School and the officers on the air staff had failed to anticipate the vulnerability of the bombers against such an efficient foe. General Donald Wilson, one of the architects of the concept of strategic bomber operations at the school, recalled that "the engineers devoted more of their attention to making the airplane go further and faster with little concern with what it was to do when it got to where it was going." He said "I think we did a lot of wishful thinking and assumed that the B-17 as it was originally designed could protect itself in the air."[6] Air Marshall Harris had tried to warn Eighth Air Force leaders that the RAF with its own heavies, including the Avro Lancaster, a four-engine bomber comparable to the B-17 and B-24, had failed at such techniques on daylight bombing missions deep into Germany. Therefore, he pleaded with American commanders to profit by British experience during the dark days of 1940 and 1941, and suggested that the Eighth follow the RAF example and bomb only at night. But Generals Spaatz and Eaker were determined to make the pre-war plans fit the situation at hand, and they were convinced that American bombers could effectively hit strategic targets through daylight precision bombing even without fighter escorts.

The American strategists also had the Norden bomb sight that they believed would make Eighth Air Force daylight bombing both practical and accurate. It had been invented by a civilian consultant to the Navy, Carl L. Norden, in 1931. The Top Secret bomb sight was superior to anything the British had, and Spaatz and Eaker believed it would be the critical difference in bombing accuracy, therefore causing the Eighth Air Force to succeed where the British had failed. In theory then, the Americans would have the essential ingredients for success—long range bombers with sufficient armament to penetrate German skies, and a bomb sight that would make daylight precision bombing a success. However, in practice, both products of pre-war engineering would come up short.

So, armed with theories, plans, bombers, and related equipment, Army Air Corps officers went to London in 1940 to observe the potential of air power during the Battle of Britain and in the London blitz that followed. In observing Hitler's effort to attempt to break the British will with attacks on London, and British retaliation against German targets, they had their first opportunity to observe two combatants attempting to defeat each other through aerial bombardment. As a result of their assessment Generals Spaatz and Eaker became even more convinced that, though the Luftwaffe failed in its efforts to break the will of the British people, and though RAF Bomber Command paid a terrible price in its attempts at daylight precision bombing of German targets, the problem was not the concept, but a lack of the right combination of tactics and equipment. Hopefully the Eighth would have both.

The attack on Pearl Harbor forced the American theorists and planners to face reality, as Britain's war suddenly became theirs. By that time, RAF Bomber Command had already discounted daylight bombing and reverted to so called nighttime "area bombing" or what some referred to as "terror bombing." In fact, just before General Eaker arrived in England to assume command of the American counterpart of the RAF Bomber Command, RAF bombing missions into the rich German industrial Ruhr Valley had convinced Harris once and for all that daylight precision bombing, whereby bombers had to fly a straight pattern through a heavy field of antiaircraft flak while fending off the Luftwaffe fighters, was just too costly to continue. British officials had come to the conclusion that with the RAF's limited amount of equipment and available bomber crews along with heavy attrition, especially on deep penetration missions into Germany, it should direct its bombs at a broader target area that included not only industrial sites but the towns in which they were located. Additional emphasis would be directed at the morale of the German citizens. Therefore, it was thought in most influential quarters both inside and outside the Air Ministry that so-called area attacks, as they then began to be called, even against targets near large centers of population, was the policy of choice...," even with the uncertainties and inaccuracies inherent in night time bombing.[7]

RAF Bomber Command Chief, Air Marshall Arthur Harris in particular, would not deviate from that approach until the final days of the war in spite of criticism from many quarters that such tactics were immoral and inhumane and resulted in countless deaths to innocent civilians. The devastation from fire bombs inflicted on cities such as Hamburg and Dresden, only added fuel to the controversy that continues to this day.

Meanwhile, in spite of British warnings, Spaatz and Eaker believed in their equipment and strategy and for various reasons, not the least of which was the moral side of the issue, they were determined to make daylight precision bombing succeed. Even with repeated requests from Harris and Prime Minister Churchill, especially in the difficult days of 1943 when the Eighth Air Force seemed to be bleeding to death, they would not deviate from the more humane strategy.

There were times in the early days of the war, when Army Air Forces officials, in particular General Arnold, questioned whether or not the American approach could do the job. Certainly that was the case in the fall and winter of 1943-1944, when losses were so heavy that deep penetration raids were put on hold until long-range fighters were available. Through incredible American development and production efforts that produced the P-51 Mustangs, and P-47 Thunderbolts with added wing tanks that could escort the bombers deep into Germany, giving the B-17s and B-24s access to targets everywhere in Hitler's Third Reich, the inadequacy in pre-war planning had finally been corrected. Then, not only did the fighters provide the critical escort role for the bombers, but in so doing also destroyed a good part of the enemy fighter force, its air fields, and its aircraft, both in the air and on the ground. Even so, the accuracy that the Eighth Air Force leaders believed to be possible never fully matched their expectations. The much heralded Norden bomb sight generally placed bombs somewhere in a 1,000 to 5,000 foot range of the target; destroying many of the target complexes, but not hitting the so-called "pickle barrel" as some had predicted.

In addition to the experienced Luftwaffe pilots, the Eighth also had to contend with the more elusive, impersonal, and certainly unpredictable flak from exploding artillery shells over target areas that never lost its effectiveness, even in the latter days of the war. Air crews were especially fearful of flak in that they could do nothing about it. All they could do was fly through it and hope that they would not be hit, especially on bomb runs where they were most vulnerable and unable to take evasive action. Lieutenant Frank Bolen, of Selma Alabama, and bombardier in the 91st Bomb Group, describes its devastating impact as his formation neared the chemical plant at Ludwigshafen Germany on June 2, 1944. "I looked ahead [and] the sky was made dark by flak bursting at the exact altitude we were flying," he said, "right in our path and directly over the target." As in thousands of other bomber formations in the skies over Europe, he had no choice but to hope and pray that the shrapnel peppering his aircraft would not deal his plane a fatal blow. Unfortunately, his worst fears were realized as his bomber was hit by one of the shells inflicting such severe damage as to leave him no choice but to bail out to be greeted by captors on the ground. While the war was over for him, the agony of confinement in Stalag Luft I was still ahead. His POW experiences are covered in chapter seven.[8]

Three months before Pearl Harbor, the Air War Plans Division in Washington prepared a planning document known as AWPD 1, which laid out the estimates of future forces needed for any foreseeable Air Force mission. That plan was revised on October 1, 1941, and along with other plans for a future war, became the subject of many discussions within the air staff. But such plans never matched the eventual requirements the Air Force would need when the real thing came along. Pre-war plans, like most plans, were in for much refinement and many were later cast aside while those that remained underwent drastic revision. The process began at the ARCADIA conference held in Washington D.C., from December 22, 1941 through January 14, 1942, between Prime Minister Churchill, President Roosevelt, and key members of their civilian and military staffs. There they developed the "European first strategy" that gave first priority for offensive action on Germany while remaining forces mounted a defensive war in the Pacific.

Air power was to be part of the strategy, with the air forces of Britain and the United States officially tasked to take the war directly to Hitler's Europe. Such operations were deemed critical in preparation for the second front, so desperately desired by their respective countries and their ally, the Soviet Union. The latter was especially anxious for a European offensive that might take some of the unrelenting pressure it faced from the still powerful Wehrmacht on the Eastern Front. Indeed, there was little good news in the war in the early spring of 1942, and the military chiefs had to parcel out the meager military forces with utmost care. In all directions from North Africa to the Pacific, the Axis powers had the upper hand.

But the implementation of effective bombing against Nazi targets was slow to come. In a real sense American "air power" did not exist in January 1942, nor did the Eighth Air Force. Both were still somewhere in the dream stage, and dependent on how fast the war industry could be geared up to meet the enormous military demands coming from every direction. Their very existence and missions during the first six months of 1942 were predicated on availability of aircraft, crews, and equipment along with the changing face of early military operations. In fact while the Eighth Air Force was established on January 28, 1942, it would not drop its first bombs on Germany until the following August. In addition to the task of attempting to meet demands for both aircraft and crews the struggling Eighth Air Force was caught in the cross currents of countless debates over correct strategy and target selection all directed at the opening of the second front. Possible dates for the D-day invasion varied from late 1942 to late 1943, and of course would eventually slip to spring of 1944. The buildup of sufficient forces in England to support the invasion came under the nickname "Operation Bolero." However, while air power was badly needed for the effort, Eighth Air Force commanders could do little in 1942 and 1943 with aircraft and crews stretched to the limit due to the loss of planes and men, first to the Pacific, second North Africa, and third Italy. Yet, it had no choice but to mount an air offensive to prepare for an amphibious invasion. As Hitler and Goering had recognized in 1940 through 1941 in their unsuccessful planning for operation "Sea Lion," control of the air was essential for any amphibious invasion and, for the allies, that meant destruction of the powerful Luftwaffe. That reality finally caused debate over which targets to hit that in turn led the Eighth to focus on one direction: destruction of German aircraft, aircraft plants, and air fields.

Remarkably, in spite of the demands placed on it during this complicated and uncertain period, the Eighth Air Force did persevere and by the summer of 1943, thanks to the efforts of determined and extremely capable airmen, was prepared to join the RAF in what would be called "round the clock bombing," with the British flying at night and Americans in the day.

But it had a most difficult and painful beginning. First, General Duncan had to move the newly manufactured bombers and green crewmen to England, in itself a daunting challenge. On February 12, 1942, in a report to General Arnold, Duncan listed the anemic Eighth Air Force inventory as of that date. It included only one medium bomb group of B-25s, and one light bomb group of obsolete DB-7s, in addition to two groups of P-39F fighters, four observation squadrons and one photo squadron. While Duncan could not predict the types or numbers of aircraft needed in the upcoming "Operation Gymnast", in North Africa, he knew the above meager aircraft and equipment were next to nothing. Therefore, with approval of the Task Force Commander for the move to Europe, Major General Lloyd R. Fredendall, he recommended a beginning Eighth Air Force of:

    3 heavy bomb groups with B-17 or B-24 planes
    2 medium bomb groups with B-25 or B-26 planes
    1 light bomb group with A-20 planes
    5 pursuit groups with P-38s, P-39s P-40s, P47s
    1 Observation Group
    1 Mapping squadron

He anticipated that the force could not be in place in less than seven months, which would be an accurate estimate for the beginning of the North African campaign. He pointed out that, even with the recommended aircraft and crews, the Eighth Air Force would have no better than a fifty- to sixty-percent chance of accomplishing its mission.[9] In short, General Duncan painted a very bleak picture of the Eighth Air Force in its infancy.

Before the bombers could even begin their treacherous trips to Britain and begin operations, Eighth Bomber Command, the bomber component of The Eighth Air Force, had to establish a headquarters along with bases for the B-17 and B-24 bombers. When plans for the second front were changed in March 1942, General Eaker,

Commander, and a small contingent of officers were already in England making preparations for deployment and arrival of the American bomber force.

On May 5, General Spaatz assumed command of the Eighth Air Force, and in August, General Eisenhower gave Spaatz the additional duties as air officer for ETOUSA (European Theater of Operations, USA), a position he would hold throughout the remainder of the war.[10] Key commanders and staff were then in place to begin bombing operations.

In the meantime General Eaker was busy working with his British counterparts preparing for the arrival of crews and aircraft. From the beginning the British were gracious and helpful in lending him the assistance he needed. Three days after his arrival, General Eaker began work with RAF Bomber Command officers for the process of training, equipping and employing American air units. On April 15, he established his permanent headquarters at High Wycombe, a former girls school in Buckinghamshire, about thirty miles west of London and about five miles from RAF Bomber Command headquarters. A story made the rounds that on the first night at High Wycombe the duty officer was plagued by the sound of bells. Upon investigation it was discovered that on the walls of the recently vacated girls school, cards were affixed which advised the girls that in the event of distress they were to "Ring twice for mistress."[11] The code word for High Wycombe was "Pinetree," a word that would become very familiar to anxious bomber crews awaiting mission assignments in the days to come.

During that difficult period of working out the many details of logistics and operations, Eaker relied heavily on British experiences, and in fact he patterned the bomber component of the Eighth Air Force, Eighth Bomber Command, after RAF Bomber Command. Accounts from those busy months indicate a maximum amount of cooperation between the two allies. While the two air forces would differ at times regarding strategy, Anglo-American relations were never any better than they were in the trying days of 1942. By May 18, Eaker was able to notify Spaatz that "the bomber headquarters should be ready to control and supervise bomber operations by the first of June."

Of course aircraft and men were the critical elements missing in those precarious days. But that began to change July 1, 1942, when the first B-17E landed at Preswick, England, and a month later the Eighth Air Force was ready to begin operations. Meanwhile, across the Atlantic, men from every state joined Alabamians on the long road that would link them to bombers and fighters as they took their place in the long history of air power.

3

Two Cultures, A Single Objective

So it is only common sense to understand that the first and major duty Hitler has given his propaganda chiefs is to separate Britain and America and spread distrust between them. If he can do so, then his chance of winning might return.
       Over There, Instructions for American Servicemen in Britain

All of a sudden the war didn't seem so far away, when we saw the personnel come in to gather up the crew's personal effects so we could have their beds.
       Samuel Ross, 384th FG

George Stebbings lived in the rich agricultural area of East Anglia known as the Little Ouse Valley, within walking distance of the small village of Knettishell. He had never seen an American until 1942 when, at the age of twelve, he witnessed the arrival of B-17s of the 388th Bomb Group. He recalls that the conversion of farm land adjacent to his home into what became Knettishell Airfield, "transformed… his life and the lives of other British citizens in that peaceful area of East Anglia in ways they never imagined. Everything appeared to be happening at twice the pace of everyday life," he said. "I was overwhelmed by the constant movement of men, machines, and vehicles of all types; an almost constant stream of takeoffs and landings; the constant throbbing of aircraft engines with their brakes screaming in protest; sounds never to be forgotten..."[1]

Ron Batley, who grew up approximately one mile from Thorpe Abbots, about an hour west of Knettishell, and home of the 100th Bomb Group, agrees with Stebbings and adds that "the effect this invasion had on the lives of local farmers and villagers lasted well past war's end. Living alongside their American allies, British civilians shared the triumphs and tragedies the war brought."[2]

Nor were their American allies anymore prepared for the cultural exchange with their new British acquaintances. They too were to have their lives transformed, not only by the hostile and unforgiving experiences of combat, but like the British, by acquaintance with a culture and form of the English language that was far removed from the world they left behind. Stebbings evaluates the mixture of the two cultures as a success and believes that "Americans of the Eighth Air Force did more than anyone, especially politicians, to bring American and British people together."[3]

The British citizens called the home of the Eighth Air Force "little America." Officially, it is East Anglia, a mostly agricultural and pastoral area that stretches from the sea to the east and northeast of London, to the combination of medieval and modern buildings of Cambridge to the west, and to the corn and wheat fields, marsh lands, manor houses, and thatch-roofed cottages of Suffolk to the south. It is the England of scenic post cards, and in its peaceful atmosphere punctuated on occasions by the sounds and sights of long-tailed, brilliantly colored pheasants or the bleating of sheep, its quaintness belies the fact that at one time thousands of bombers disturbed its serenity as instruments of war, the likes of which the British people had never known.

East Anglia encompasses an area about half the size of the state of Vermont, and yet from 1942 to 1945, along with a smaller area to its west referred to as the Midlands, housed some sixty-five American air fields from which the heavy bombers, along with single engine fighter escorts, flew daily missions over Hitler's Fortress Europe. Along with some 700 other airfields crammed into England, the British and their American cousins launched every type of mission, from fighter support and bombing of strategic targets, to troop transport.

To many Eighth Air Force crews, East Anglia would be a most welcome sight after their bombers, many with engines out or windmilling, shattered tail sections and, fuel nearly exhausted, successfully limped over the White Cliffs of Dover following the horror they had just witnessed over the continent of Europe.

In addition to the Eighth Air Force, the Ninth Air Force was located in Southern and Eastern England to support the D-day operations, while the Fifteenth Air Force operated out of North Africa and Italy, thereby providing combined coverage of the entire European theatre The experiences of Eighth Air Force personnel were repeated many times over by the heroic men of those air forces. Include the hundreds of Royal Air Force missions and wartime Britain was a maze of activity on the ground and in the air like no other military venture in the history of warfare. One description of wartime Britain dotted by air fields in every direction was of an "island that had a bad case of measles."[4]

Eighth Air Force airfield construction began in 1942 on some 8,000 miles of prime agricultural land either lent to the Americans by British landlords or confiscated by the government. It was the largest single building project in British history. The cost of each completed airfield was estimated at four million dollars or by twenty-first century value, $150 million. Both East Anglian and Midland sites were well suited for airfield construction. They were level in most places with no spot more than 400 feet above sea level. By late 1943 a traveler through the area would have found an airfield ten miles or less from any single point. Both fighter and bomber bases were similar in layout. Each occupied approximately 500 acres of land, and generally had a distinctive pattern of three 150-foot-wide intersecting runways in lengths ranging from 6,000 feet, the main runway, to 3,000 feet for the subsidiary runways. A fifty-foot-wide perimeter track provided access to all parts of the field. Some fifty hard stands (paved aircraft parking areas) dotted areas adjacent to the perimeter track, and each field also had two or three large hangars, a control tower, and a full technical site for maintenance and support activities.

Living quarters for approximately 3,000 personnel were located on or around each base. Crews lived in hastily constructed wooden buildings, or more likely, small Nissen or Quonset huts usually made of steel and capable of holding from eight to twenty men. William Dupree describes his quarters at Seething, a B-24 base and home of the 448th Bomb Group, located about 15 miles south of Norwich: "There were two flight crews per hut. Officers were in one area and enlisted men in another area. In those [Quonset] huts were metal double deck beds, one mattress, four blankets along with one small coal stove centrally located. Coal allowance was a bucket per day, plus what we could steal from the dining hall coal bin. We would put coal in our pockets when we went to chow. A tomato can, suspended by a coat hanger in the stove, served as a pot to boil eggs in for a special treat. Every station was self sufficient with water storage facilities, electrical generating equipment, and sewage disposal."[5]

Thorpe Abbotts, home of the 100th Bomb Group, was typical both in facilities and rural surroundings. It was located on the edge of a little medieval village by the same name, with access to the base by a quaint country lane bordered by pasture land and wheat fields. In addition to living quarters, the base had mess halls, recreation facilities, sick quarters, and other amenities to make life between missions as pleasant as possible. Since the barracks were located too far from base operations for easy walking, bicycles were an essential part of every airman's personal belongings, creating a virtual jungle of the two wheelers traveling along the perimeter in and out of the base and accumulating in jangled piles in front of operations. Like so many other bases, trees encircled the field, and always caused apprehension when heavily loaded bombers strained to go airborne, often using every foot of runway. Other base facilities were adjacent to the perimeter track on the opposite side of the airfield from the control tower. Harry Crosby, Navigator in the 100th Bomb Group, recalls his first glimpse of the air field when he arrived there in May 1943: "We were on a big farm," he said. "We saw a farmer out in the field with a team of horses. There were several homes right on the base. At first we didn't see any Americans and then, on the right, a cluster of low, long Nissen huts and a group of GIs in fatigues playing catch and hitting at each other. ... After another hundred yards we saw cows going through the squadron yard."[6]

Construction of the air base at Levenham, ten miles South East of Bury St Edmunds, and about sixty miles northeast of London, home of the 487th Bombardment Group, was typical of the process by which farm land was converted to war use. In 1943, the British Air Ministry requested the owner of 250 acres of the David Alston's Lodge Farm to sell the land for the air base. The original owner's son, David, remembers that his father decided that he wouldn't sell the land, but would give it to them for the duration of the war as his contribution to the war effort. It was "on the agreement that the moment peace was declared, the land would revert to him." The Air Ministry also permitted the family to stay on the farm, thus contrasting the very familiar pastoral scene of a farmer working the land and tending the crops next door to the instruments of war with their thundering engines noisily indicating their presence day and night.

When the construction crew completed their work at the end of March 1944, the sprawling military facility literally surrounded Lodge Farm. On April 4, 1944, B-24s of the 487th Bombardment Group began arriving at the base, designated Army Air Force Station 137. The farmhouse stood only 350 yards away from one runway, 400 yards away from base headquarters, and 150 yards from the hard stands. Alston echoed a remark made by many tenants of the converted farm land: "They used to warm up every morning about five o'clock for about half an hour," he said. "Eventually, the family grew accustomed to it."[7]

About 20 miles northeast of Levenham, nine-year-old Sam Hurry watched the nine-month construction of Thorpe Abbotts followed by the arrival of the first forty-two bombers. Like many other young men living near the bases, Hurry wasted no time in meeting the new neighbors. "They ran errands for the airmen, and earned extra money by taking their laundry home for their mothers to do," he said.[8] They developed friendships with the crews that continue to this day.

The first Eighth Air Force bombers arrived in the newly constructed air fields in the spring of 1942. Their trip across the hazardous Atlantic took one of two forms. Many airmen joined the thousands of other anxious and nervous European-bound servicemen and endured the choppy seas and submarine-infested waters aboard troop ships. On January 10, 1944, Red Harper of the 100th Bomb Group, together with 1,500 Air Force personnel and sixteen thousand other troops, departed New York on an old French luxury liner, "Isle d`France," for the nine-day turbulent journey to Scotland. He had the typical experience of "crowded conditions, terrible food, and much sea sickness. The ship changed course and speed every three minutes to avoid the U-boats." In addition to his seasickness, Harper remembers his apprehension when "it was rumored there was room in the life boats for only fifteen to eighteen hundred men" out of eighteen thousand total. Somehow the math did not seem to work in his favor. The rumor came to mind on his first night when he spotted what he thought was a periscope in the water. He was much relieved when a ship's officer informed him that it was a friendly submarine.[9]

Howard Polin of the 352nd Fighter Group experienced a slightly different but no less grueling situation on the H.M.S. Morton Bay, an old meat packing ship, that had gone to sea for the first time back in 1898. The ship departed New York on March 10, 1944, and arrived at Cardiff, Wales, on March 22. He slept in a hammock strung between two meat hooks. The old relic of the Spanish American War sailed in a fifty-ship convoy with destroyers for protection. He got his first glimpse of war as one ship was hit by a German U-boat. Like Harper, he remembers the zigzagging that kept the latrines busy with seasick troops.[10] Guy Cofield, of the 379th Bomb Group, recalls the horrible food on his trip aboard an old converted Scandinavian cargo ship. In desperation he managed to improve on his diet somewhat by volunteering to work in the officer's mess. When he was not working, he stayed on deck to escape the heat and crowded conditions.[11]

Most European bound airmen took an even more dangerous route across the Atlantic and ferried new B-17s or B-24s to Britain to add to the rapidly expanding inventory of bombers. Such trips were rife with danger, and many bombers never made it to Britain. In fact many Eighth Air Force personnel look back on the trip across the Atlantic as one of their most difficult and horrifying experiences. Gerald Astor, *The Mighty Eighth,* was quite accurate in describing the trip to the United Kingdom as "almost akin to the earliest voyages against the uncharted Atlantic 450 years earlier, although Columbus at least knew enough to sail through the climes rather than the slower and much less forgiving North Atlantic."[12]

Benton White's trip was typical. He and the other nine men in his crew picked up a new B-17 at Kearney, Nebraska, and began their trans-ocean trip across the Atlantic at Manchester, New Hampshire. From there they flew some one thousand miles to Goose Bay, Labrador, where they landed in snow up to wing tip level. Then they endured unfriendly weather conditions on the 1,700 mile leg of their trip to Reykjavik, Iceland. After awaiting clear weather they left for Prestwick, Scotland, where they turned in their bomber to the supply depot and made their way to a replacement depot for assignment to a bomber group.[13]

Quitman Hurdle, of the 392nd Bomb Group, took another much used route. He began in Florida and then flew the southern route first to Puerto Rico, then to Brazil, on to Ascension Island in the South Pacific, then to Bacar, Africa, before finally landing in Ireland. Weather conditions, difficulty in navigating, and some anxious moments concerning their rapidly shrinking fuel capacity made the friendly Irish base a most welcome site. On a similar route, B-24 bombardier Lawson Corley of the 446th Bomb Group, was awaiting departure in Bacar when he was spurred by a buzzard; a wound that would cause him difficulty for years to come.[14] As the crews landed safely, they were often heard to comment: "It can't be much worse than what we just went through." They were wrong!

After reaching Britain either by troop ship or bomber, the new arrivals headed for one of several replacement depots. In most instances they went by train, often at night, with windows covered to avoid becoming a target for enemy aircraft; their first taste of the realities of wartime England. Following processing, the crews were usually split up for orientation on their respective positions in their bombers, gunners going to one location, bombardiers and navigators to another, and pilots to another.

Harper recalls his arrival in England and the trip from his port at Firth of Clyde, Scotland, in route to Thorpe Abbotts. From there he traveled by train to Stone, a small town near Liverpool, to await his assignment while sampling the peculiarities of the British culture. He had heard about British pub life and was anxious to "test the waters." On his first night he satisfied his curiosity by visiting a pub closest to the processing center. He remembered that "the main beverage was a type of beer the British called 'stout' that came straight from a huge barrel at room temperature. It was not carbonated like American beer and it took some getting used to...maybe 20 minutes at the most." British tradition for the natives who went "pub crawling" was to sit and nurse a pint for an hour or so. "They were appalled to see the guys from the 'colonies' guzzle down maybe six pints of the stuff during their one," he said.[15]

Bovington, near London, was the replacement center for many of the pilots. Harper recalls that since the base was close to London, he could see the "flash and hear the boom of the Nazi bombs being dropped on the nightly bombing of the historic city." Most of the instructors were seasoned RAF veterans who had experienced combat during the worst days of the Battle of Britain. They were part of the "few" who remained from RAF Squadrons that had been decimated by the best the Luftwaffe could offer. They knew the Luftwaffe pilots very well, and were well qualified to acquaint the new crews not only with the peculiarities associated with flying in and around England but also with accounts of their first-hand experiences with the tenacious enemy they would soon face. The veterans also were aware that the confident Americans, so enamored with the much publicized firepower and defensive capability of the B-17s and B-24s, were in for a difficult time attempting daylight precision bombing.

Harper had arrived in January 1944, a time when the certainty of victory by either the RAF or Eighth Air Force was very much in doubt, and the many vacant chairs in the British mess hall attested to that sad reality. Following orientation, the crews received their group assignments and boarded the train again, this time destined for their bases in either East Anglia or the Midlands.[16]

In reflecting on their journey by train to their new home the airmen remember that their first impression of East Anglia was an area similar to countless rural areas of America, but on a much smaller scale. The quaint houses with their thatched roofs and villages were small by American standards, and with their medieval appearance and modest size and style obviously belonged to a bygone era. When they arrived at rail stations not far from their destination, they were normally met by base personnel in a 6x6 (wheel base) truck for transportation to the air field. That trip varied in distance from approximately two to ten miles, and as the truck traveled down the narrow country road and entered the base with all the trappings of war, the new arrivals were quickly aware of the stark contrast between the world they had left behind and one they had entered. As they looked about at the olive drab structures, and listened to the roar of engines being tested, or the sound of aircraft overhead, World War II was no longer just a distant conflict far removed from the peaceful lives of their homeland. When Walter Fleming joined the 487th Bomb Group, at Lavingham, July 29, 1944, he knew the war was real when a German buzz bomb exploded about 500 yards from the Quonset hut in which he had just taken up residence. As in some dream with a well-crafted script that had no apparent ending, he knew he had left the quaintness of England behind and had taken his place on the stage of a real life drama. His former life as a coal miner in Alabama seemed very far away.[17]

Along with other advice his British instructors gave him, Harper recalls being advised to try to avoid assignment to the 100th Bomb Group at Thorpe Abbotts, referred to as the "bloody 100th," due to its many losses of planes and crews. Unfortunately, assignment officials paid little attention to his personal desires, and he was shocked to learn that he was destined for the 100th. He recalled that his uneasy feelings toward his assignment were only intensified by the daily scenes of planes coming over his training center headed North, in the direction of Thorpe Abbotts, some with props feathered, others trailing smoke, and some firing red-flares to signify priority landing because of wounded aboard. One had only half a stabilizer but still kept its place in the formation.[18]

After a few days of orientation and combat training Harper took the train to the little town of Diss, a few miles from Thorpe Abbotts. Arriving at night with windows covered, he had no concept of what East Anglia was like until he disembarked at the Diss train station. Then he suddenly found himself in what appeared to be a time warp. Diss predated the founding of America and the lifestyle had not changed much over the years. While the town had been ravaged by the plague in 1579, and by fire in 1640, it still retained its ancient buildings. When air crews from surrounding bases visited the town on days off, they ate at the seventeenth century Greyhound Inn, and on Friday, which was market day, shopped in the quaint shops.

Whether visiting the ancient pubs, shopping, or visiting the thousand-year-old parish church, airmen were astonished not only at the contrast with life "back home," but also the contrast of life as usual in towns like Diss, with the grim reality of the war that hung over the base and seemed to permeate every waking thought.

Following his arrival at Thorpe Abbotts, Harper was assigned to a building with two other crews. As he settled in, he spotted four empty cots. They had been occupied previously by a Lieutenant Fletcher and other officers in his crew before their mission to Brunswick, a subsequent crash landing in Holland, and probable internment by the Germans, a sobering greeting for these "green" airmen who had never tasted combat. As was the custom, all evidence of the former crew's existence was removed, and their names were no longer mentioned; one more somber reminder of the ominous future he faced.[19]

Each officer had a wooden dresser with a large mirror on top of it. Then another sobering incident. He was told to prepare a "just in case" letter and to place it at the corner of the mirror. The letter contained a message to a loved one stating that "receipt of the letter was an indication that the writer had been shot down and there was a better-than-even chance that he would be a prisoner of the Germans for the duration of the war." Of course receipt of the letter was also cause for grief by the recipient when death had been confirmed. Unfortunately, for men of the 100th Bomb Group, too many of the letters were mailed in the course of the air war, and too many cots were vacated after missions, some for the second, third, or more times.[20]

Samuel Ross, ball turret gunner in the 384th Bomb Group at Grafton Underwood Air Base, about 80 miles north of London, along with five enlisted men in his crew, followed a normal procedure of temporary assignment of about forty men to a barracks awaiting a crew vacancy—usually from a combat loss. Unfortunately, they did not wait long. A few days after their arrival a vacancy occurred that in turn gave his crew a permanent assignment to a combat position. "All of a sudden the war didn't seem so far away," he said, "when we saw the personnel come in to gather up the crew's personal effects so we could have their beds."[21]

White's experience in April 1944 was similar to Harper's in that he, his copilot, and his pilot, went by train to the little town of Hemel

Hempstead, north of London, for processing and ground training. He remembers that the train windows were also covered, and all of the towns along the way were blacked out. Like Harper, he recalls the sounds and sights of the nightly bombing of London. In fact he was so close to the action he could see the search lights crisscrossing the night sky and the images of German bombers on the nightly Luftwaffe raids. It was quite a welcome for a young pilot who only a year earlier had been most worried about preparing for final exams at Auburn University. After several weeks of training, he was assigned to the 94th Bomb Group at Bury St Edmunds, about seventy miles north of London.[22]

By mid-1943, replacements were arriving at the bases in a steady flow. Ben White, Henry Arnold, and Roy Davidson were among that group. All remember the feelings they had in leaving the train at the Bury St Edmunds station to find themselves stepping back into the Middle Ages. Bury St Edmunds was once visited by Charles Dickens who described it in *Pickwick Papers* as "a handsome little town of thriving and cleanly appearance." In the center of the town are the remains of what was, from 633A.D. until its destruction by fire in 1327, one of the most spectacular monasteries and abbeys in all of England. The plaque at its entrance read that in 1214 barons gathered at the high alter of the abbey to force King John to grant the Magna Carta. How appropriate that the birth place of the document that began the long process of democracy was next door to the place where young men would give their lives to help preserve its heritage. To add to the roots of the America they left behind, the airmen had only to travel about ten miles west of Bury St Edmunds to Thetford and the former home of American patriot Thomas Paine, then being used as a pub and hotel. How ironic that the home of a man who at one time poured out his wrath on the King of England in his famous political treatise, *Common Sense,* had been converted to a pub used by airmen willing to sacrifice their lives to save twentieth-century England.

The War Department did all that it could to prepare Americans for what they could expect in Britain. A pamphlet, *Instructions for American Servicemen in Britain 1942*, gave the following introduction to the newly arriving servicemen and some advice:

"You are going to Great Britain as part of an Allied offensive-to meet Hitler and beat him on his own ground. For the time being you will be Britain's guest. The purpose of this guide is to start getting you acquainted with the British, their country, and their ways.

America and Britain are allies. Hitler knows that they, with the other united nations, mean his crushing defeat in the end.

So it is only common sense to understand that the first and major duty Hitler has given his propaganda chiefs is to separate Britain and America and spread distrust between them. If he can do so, his chance of winning might return."[23]

The British hosts were both curious and friendly as they sized up these cousins from abroad. George Stebbings described his relations with Americans as "one great adventure." He was fascinated by the variety of foreign-sounding names. He said "I was accustomed to English family names unchanged through the centuries." In one of his earliest encounters with the air crews, he remembered watching the men gambling "and losing more money in a single evening than he had seen in his life time." To many of the locals, all Americans were "very rich." The crews also enjoyed using Stebbings as a listening board for their exploits both in combat and in their social life. He recalled "listening to ground crews in particular, discuss their leaves and visits to London , and their various adventures with the good time girls, so-called Piccadilly commandoes, or how they were rebuked by local girls who refused to accept their advances," heavy stuff for a twelve year old. "All of the air crews he personally knew returned safely from their missions," he said, and he "believed they looked at him as providing good luck." He was also impressed with their "enthusiasm for their aircraft." His most memorable experiences came when the crews allowed him to fly on twenty illegal training flights in B-17s. "Every day was a new experience," he says, and like other youth on other bases he believed "that the bombers and bases would always be there."[24]

Cliff Hall remembers his experiences on the base at Bury St Edmunds, when as a young lad of twelve, he watched the transformation of the fertile farm land adjacent to his father's farm into an air base, and then the arrival of the first air crews and B-17s. Hall regularly rode his bicycle to the base, and made it a point to get to know as many crews as possible. Like Stebbings and other youth near air bases, he became their go-between with farmers who would sell fresh eggs or other items to crews. Hall did have some painful memories such as a crash at the end of the runway with no survivors. On another occasion he saw a crippled B-17 land with wounded and dead crew members. After looking at the carnage in the plane he avoided meeting any other returning bombers. For two exciting years he considered the men of the 94th Bomb Group as "his family," and with a voice that momentarily chokes and appears to drift off as he recalls so many memories of the life he lived sixty years ago, his one comment concerning the end of the war and the return of the base to farm land was "I lost all me friends."[25]

Another youngster, Bill Sharpe, lived next door to Atcham, a fighter base located in the Midlands, near the town of Shrewsbury. He remembers learning so much about Americans he had never known before, and in particular being introduced to peanut butter, a real delicacy. His parents provided the Americans with eggs, English beer, and other items, and his mother did their laundry. He estimates that he made about fifty trading visits to the base.[26]

Hilburn F. Richards, B-24 Aircraft Commander, 492nd Bomber Group, at Cheddington, about a hundred miles North of London, recalls the pleasant times he had with families that regularly invited him to their church services followed by dinner. The British were a "strong, fearless, stalwart people," he says. He remembers how accustomed the British were to the reality of the war they had endured for almost five years. He was especially impressed that they did not panic at the sight of V-1 bombs hitting close by.[27]

Frank Bolen, described the people near Bassingbourne, southwest of Cambridge, and home of the 91st Bomb Group, as "basically good with widespread acceptance on both sides." He remembered "lots of parties, pubs, dances, and other types of entertainment to satisfy participants. Animosities were few and insignificant,"[28] he said. A British Women's Volunteer Service worker remembers the buzz of excitement when she and her colleagues heard the news of "the friendly invasion of some 1,000 American troops, our allies ... Ideas as to what would best make them happy were conflicting ... This was our first opportunity of repaying the U.S.'s fabulous generosity, and we seemed to be anxious to the point of hysteria for them to like us."[29]

Many British people looked at the whole experience as "good as tonic." In a war that seemed endless and sometimes hopeless, a Red Cross worker in Norwich believed that the GIs "brought with them color, romance, warmth and a tremendous hospitality to our dark, shadowed island."[30]

Upon their arrival in England, Americans were warned that they would encounter living conditions and an overall lifestyle that had been greatly changed as a result of years of war. "Britain may look a little shop worn and grimy to you," they were warned, but "the British are anxious to have you know that you are not seeing their country at its best." Even late in the war when they left an America that was really beginning to feel the effect of rationing, they were shocked at the contrast of the British living conditions with those in the world they left behind.

Glenn Taylor, 466th Bomb Group at Atlebridge located eight miles NW of Norwich, found the people to be "poorly dressed, and with bad teeth." He was invited to a home for Sunday lunch and described the meal as "probably the worst meal I had in England, due to their rationing of food." But Taylor, like other Alabamians accepting British hospitality, realized the people were giving the best they had. He was warned that when invited to a British home to "go easy" when the host told him "to eat up there's plenty on the table." It was probably the family's entire ration for the week.[31]

The average British family received a weekly meat ration of two small lamb chops and four ounces of bacon, and even that meager amount was not always available at the local butcher shop. The British woman made do with one drab dress every nine months and a new nightgown every four years. Even Bronco toilet paper, coarse by American standards, was scarce. The British shopper could always expect long queues and often empty shelves for most consumer items.

On occasion, local residents would invite the airmen to their homes for relaxation and temporary respite from the military environment. On one such occasion, Guy Cofield, of the 379th Bomb Group at Kimboltin, remembers a highlight of his time in England as "being invited to have poached eggs by a local family, a real treat after eating powdered eggs for many months that bounced when they flopped into your mess kit." James Ritchie, Intelligence Officer, in the 447th Bomb Group, Rattlesden, described the "locals" as "friendly and sharing. I luckily had an English farm wife to do my laundry," he said, "and we kept her husband in pipe tobacco and we enjoyed bootleg eggs."[32]

Charles Gay, of the 305th Bomb Group, at Chelveston in the Midlands just east of East Anglia, described his typical experience with local citizens: "We sometimes traded cigarettes for fresh eggs. We helped our neighboring farmer harvest his grain in late summer of 1944. He had nothing but hand scythes and rakes." Gay also remembers the young boys of the nearby village as regular Sunday visitors. "They knew we got our soap, cigarettes, and candy ration that day." He was impressed with the fact that the twelve year olds knew as much about Alabama as he did.[33]

One of Richard's warmest memories was Christmas 1944 when a local family invited him and his copilot to Christmas dinner and served them the best they had.[34] Howard Polin, at Bodney Aerodrome, near Kings Lynn, shared Richard's memory and especially visits from the kids on Christmas when they fed them cake, ice cream, candy and other treats that had long been absent from the fare in their homes, creating memories that would remain with both the giver and recipient for a lifetime.[35]

Early in their tours, most Airmen were given a much appreciated three-day pass to allow them to escape the daily routine of war. A visit to London was usually at the top of their list, and fortunately, in spite of wartime conditions, the trains continued to run. When they arrived in London, they had no difficulty finding both the opportunity for rest and entertainment.

The most popular destination for officers was the Grosvenor House hotel located around the corner from the U.S. Embassy. It was nicknamed "Willow Run" after the huge B-24 Aircraft plant in Michigan. At its peak the hotel served some seven thousand meals a day. The area surrounding the hotel was a real slice of Americana, with uniforms visible in every direction. Nearby South Audley Street with its array of shopping opportunities and restaurants was described by some as a "miniature Fifth Avenue." It even had its own

PX where the GI could buy many goods not available to the average British citizen.[36]

Polin was especially impressed with the efforts of the Red Cross in London to help take their minds off the war by providing sleeping quarters and tickets to theaters, dances etc. The Red Cross headquarters was conveniently located across from Piccadilly Circus, about two miles from Covent Garden and the theater district. He recalls that the Royal Opera House was turned into a huge ballroom where big bands frequently played, and the uniform was the admission. "Girls came by subway from all over London to dance with the GIs," he said.[37]

Many Americans, especially those who had never drifted far from their hometown, looking back to their first trip to London, describe the city as overwhelming with sights they had read about, but never expected to see. They were content to go the tourist route and spent most of their time visiting such sites as the Tower of London, Trafalgar Square, Buckingham Palace, Hyde Park, or just watching the throngs of people milling around Piccadilly Circus. At entertainment sites, especially Covent Garden and at the theaters, they could for a brief few moments forget the scenes of war they had already witnessed and would see again upon return to their bases. However, one experience not high on their list was eating in London restaurants. Except for fish and chips, which were always good, they found very little on the menu that could match the chow hall on their respective bases.

Bill Varnedoe of the 385th Bomb Group located at Great Ashfield, 10 miles East of Bury St Edmunds, was given a three-day pass to London prior to his first combat mission. He realized what the British had been going through on his first night in London when he experienced the darkness of London during a blackout. He remembered, "One could stand at Piccadilly Circus and see absolutely nothing, just hear the incessant clacking of wooden heels as people walked about. One could barely make out the features of the Piccadilly Commandoes, (girls, so called because of their aggressiveness)."[38] Polin remembers that it was so dark that the more enterprising Piccadilly commandoes approached the GI and felt the insignia on his uniform to determine whether he was enlisted or officer in order to solicit the most profitable customer.[39]

While London was the place to visit and have a good time, the best relations with the British were made in close proximity to the bases. There, the British understood what the young men were going through, having already endured painful experiences of fighting a war even before the Americans came. They had suffered losses in their own neighborhoods and on distant battlefields. The GIs were reminded that while America was a country "at war" England was a "war zone" and had been so since 1939. Therefore, they could expect "great changes in the British way of life."[40]

Yet the British knew, Stebbings remembered, that "America was the one country that would bring the war to a victorious conclusion." They also knew that the young Americans were putting their lives on the line each day just as the young men of Britain had done since 1939. In most cases they were close enough to the flight line of the local base to be awakened in the morning to the roar of bomber or fighter engines, and as they worked their fields in the afternoon, they took the time to count the planes in the formation. They saw gaps in the formation or saw smoke trailing from the aircraft engines, or flares signaling wounded aboard. They often knew personally the ones who did not come back and the ones who were wounded. Death in war, whether on the battlefield or on the home front, guarantees a type of camaraderie among survivors seldom experienced in any other endeavor.[41]

Each Eighth Air Force Base was normally home for one bomb group of some thirty to fifty aircraft, depending on their type and the time in the war. For each mission the group would typically put around thirty bombers in the air in three squadrons of ten bombers each. The bombers flew in a tight formation with very little space between aircraft and no room for error.

In effect, the squadron became both the home and the family for the airmen in the Eighth, whether they were operational crew members or ground crews. They lived together, and for those who flew the missions, fought together. They experienced a closeness that few in the world back home could understand, a closeness that would forever be part of their memory. It began with their arrival at their base and assignment to their squadron and aircraft crew, and very often ended in sorrow.

After reporting for duty, the crew went through several days of training and orientation prior to their first mission. This preparation varied in length according to the phase of the war at the time they arrived. In mid-1944 the desperate need for crews caused training to become a very hurried process. Training for crews consisted of familiarity with formation flying, with emphasis on flying tight formations, while their experienced teachers taught them the peculiarities and hazards associated with combat situations to include Luftwaffe tactics and escape and evasion procedures in the event they were shot down over enemy territory. Finally the crew took its final orientation flight and was then ready to go to war.

The American Red Cross also played an important role in the everyday base life of the airmen. For example, in June 1944, the Red Cross chapter at Bury St Edmunds reported a typical month's activities. They included "weekly visits to the field and station hospitals and the base dispensary, serving sandwiches and a beverage to combat crews upon their return from missions over enemy territory, weekly programs of classical recordings, a party for those men who celebrate their birthdays in June, five softball games between 'Brooklyn Dodgers' and teams representing other squadrons and units on the field, biweekly appearance of artists from ARC-UK-HQ Entertainment Department ..., a dance, and catering to small parties given by servicemen. The report mentioned many other types of activities that were greatly appreciated by the crews. One of the popular activities was a "fish and friendship" party, in which fish was served by Red Cross Personnel. The monthly report to Red Cross Headquarters stated that "These parties have proven most successful—the men are so delighted to again experience with women, a meal, home-cooked and served with feminine care." Red Cross clubs also made holidays special occasions, doing all that they could to fill the void that such days created in home sick young men.[42]

In December of 1943, the Red Cross at Bury St Edmunds and a committee of officers and enlisted men hosted a Christmas party for "war orphans." They donated candy, cookies, and chewing gum from a week's rations for the occasion. The children were brought by truck from two different schools and entertained in one of the large hangars. They were thrilled to see Father Christmas come down the runway in a B-17. Then they went to the base Aero Club for a program of music followed by a roast pheasant dinner that concluded with sweets and ice cream, without doubt the best meal they had consumed since during the war, or among the youngest, their lives. Following an afternoon of music and entertainment Father Christmas presented each child with gifts and more sweets. This occasion was widely publicized by the BBC and the *Bury Free Press* as well as by the American Red Cross Correspondents. One base official stated that, "this party was really our Christmas, as far as real joy was concerned."[43]

The Red Cross also reported that the airmen were very much involved in all community activities and praised the relations with the English people. Many of the airmen found a welcome in local church groups such as "Church of England (Anglican), Catholic, Free Church, and Salvation Army meetings.[44] The Coney Weston Church, circa 1086, situated between several bases in the County of Suffolk, was a favorite of many airmen, especially during late 1943 and the spring of 1944 when missions were taking such a deadly toll. The congregation of this small Anglican Church never forgot the men who worshiped there and after the war erected a war memorial in honor of the Eighth Air Force personnel who shared their worship, sometimes their last, with them.

What the Red Cross did for the air crews on bases, the English pub did for them in the local community. Eighth Air Force GIs had many interesting stories about this British institution. They were always welcome as long as they remembered one thing. They were reminded in orientation literature that the pub was the "poor man's club," and "the neighborhood or village gathering place, where the men have come to see friends, not strangers."[45] Fortunately the airmen quickly learned pub etiquette, and did not remain strangers very long.

Every base was within a short bicycle ride of such a pub, and Charles Gay saw such visits as a wonderful opportunity to get to know the British people. "We frequented the Swan, a rural pub, to play darts, or cards, or just socialize," he said.[46] Some airmen such as Glenn Taylor, stationed near the village of Attlebridge, could never get use to the warm beer and consequently did very little "bar-hopping."[47] One of the favorite and most interesting pubs was The Eagle in downtown Cambridge. The Eagle had been a favorite among the pilots at Duxford during the Battle of Britain, and many used candles to burn their names into the ceiling. Frank Bolen remembered it as one of his favorites and spent much of his off time there. Americans followed the RAF tradition, and today, some sixty years later, their names on the ceiling are preserved alongside the names of the legendary pilots of the Battle of Britain.[48]

All of the experiences on and around the bases were aimed at keeping the crews' minds off the realities of the next day's mission. Unlike any other branch of service, the Eighth Air Force personnel faced the enormous contrasts between the quaint life in the British pubs and communities that reminded them of the other world they came from, and the dramatic, often deadly experiences that awaited them on the missions that had to follow. It was often difficult for the mind to adjust to such drastic extremes in that there seemed to be so many contradictions, with peace one day and war the next; life without fear in the hospitable British homes, followed by confrontation with an enemy seeking to kill them if possible.

The most significant event in an Eighth Air Force airman's life was the preparation for the more deadly of the two extremes—the missions. All thoughts of the more tranquil life were put on hold the day before a mission was to be flown, when an airman's squadron was put "on alert." If the mission was still on in the evening, the bar would close early in order for the crews to get to bed early. John Hard of the 100th Bomb Group describes the morning routine on mission day: "On mission day, we would be rousted from our beds around four a.m. We learned to dress warmly since the skies over Germany at thirty thousand feet were often a frigid fifty to sixty degrees below zero, and the B-17 was not an insulated plane. I would first don underwear, then put on a pair of olive drab pants and shirt, and finally a leather fleece-lined flying suit. I would wear two pairs of socks in low cut oxford-type shoes and put my flying boots on over that. We wore leather flying helmets with radio receivers in the ear sections, then heavy flying goggles, and at altitude, would wear oxygen masks. With our heavy flying gloves, there was not an inch of exposed skin." Breakfast was the first activity of the long day and at times was a harbinger of what was ahead. If they got real eggs instead of powdered eggs, they knew they were in for a rough day. Therefore, Hard said, "we viewed the real eggs with mixed emotions."[49] Other crews remembered that the coffee seemed to be better than usual on long mission days. However, they had to drink it sparingly, since the trip to the relief tube could be a cold venture on long missions.

After breakfast the men filed into the briefing session which was usually located in a long Quonset hut with a large covered map stretched across the front of the room. The anxious crews scramble for a seat, wide awake, anxiety fixed on their faces, wondering would the mission be a "milk run" or the other kind? Hard continues, "after all the crews were in place, our C.O., a 27-year old bird colonel …would get up and announce, your target for today is… He would pull the curtain back showing a string leading from our base at Thorpe Abbotts across the North Sea and into Germany." That part of the briefing always brought groans increasing in severity in proportion to how deep into Germany the bombers would fly—or how far they would have to contend with the Luftwaffe. The briefing officer would then tell the men which squadron would lead, assembly points for their formations, and what they could expect in flak concentrations or enemy fighters. Next he would show them the I.P. (Initial Point) which would be the beginning of the bomb run. The bomb run was usually fifty or sixty miles long, and during that time, the squadron had to be in close formation with no evasive action of any kind." During those stressful minutes the crew would only hope and pray that the impartial flak did not hit their aircraft.[50]

Following the briefing and the tense moments that followed, every member of the crew had his duties to perform as well as drawing personal equipment from supply for the mission and going to the plane to check it out. There they were greeted by the ground crew that had been working most of the night to prepare the B-17 for the crew's arrival and were still meticulously checking and rechecking every moving function of the bomber. They were very serious about their work, and would not break their concentration until the heavily loaded bomber thundered down the runway, cleared any obstacles, and lifted into the British sky. Walter Fleming, flight engineer in the 487th Bomb Group, describes the final ritual prior to boarding the aircraft: "Then we dressed for flight. First, an electrically heated suit, fleece lined boots, heated gloves, a flak jacket (steel plates sewn in canvas fabric), parachute harness, a Mae West flotation vest…A throat mike was wrapped around our neck.

Movement was limited by the electric cord to the heated suit, the communication cord and the oxygen hose."[51]

In the meantime the navigators and bombardiers had separate briefings on navigation to the target, landmarks to look for, and how to identify the primary target. William Dupree remembers the events that followed as "dramatic, noisy, and tense. We were shuttled to the ship by a GI truck, then [followed] visual inspection of the ship, props manually pulled through several cycles and then to the cockpit." As take-off time approached, the pilot started the engines and at the appointed time taxied out to the runway. All planes would assume their position in the formation according to where they would be flying. When the planes were in position the tower would fire a flare and the lead bomber would start its take off followed by the remainder of the group at thirty-second intervals.[52] As the heavily loaded bomber taxied down the runway, crews remember that brief period before it cleared the runway as one of the most frightening moments of every mission. Most crew members either witnessed or heard accounts of bombers that did not make it into the air and plunged into the ground killing the entire crew.

Eighth Air Force crewmen expected to follow the tense routine at least twenty-five, and by late 1944, thirty-five or more times before completing his tour. If all went well he could expect to go home after his designated missions. Unfortunately practically ever combat tour was iffy at best, and many crews saw the number cut short by events that took them to a German prison, a military hospital, or worse. More than twenty-five thousand experienced the worst! Virtually every airman can recount near death experiences that created memories permanently etched into his mind.

4

An Uncertain Beginning

We paid a price for the air.
General Jimmie Doolittle

On August 17, 1942, twelve B-17s of the 97th Bomb Group, Eighth Air Force, took off from Molesworth air field, about 75 miles northeast of London, crossed the English Channel, and bombed the rail marshaling yards at Rouen-Sotteville, France. Four RAF fighter squadrons escorted the bombers to their target. While the bomber force successfully hit on or around the target it did little damage to the marshaling yards. Fortunately, no bombers were lost, and when they returned to Molesworth just before dusk, the Eighth Air Force had completed its first bombing mission. For American air commanders Generals Ira Eaker and Carl (Tooey) Spaatz, that first mission was significant far beyond the slight damage to the target. It was both a major milestone in the heritage of air power that went back almost three decades, and though insignificant in results, a harbinger of what was to come.

When General Eaker addressed a British audience in March 1942, he told them that "We won't do much talking until we've done more fighting. When we leave, I hope you'll be glad we came." But the mission to nearby France and the safe return of twelve B-17s to Molesworth was hardly the "fighting" he meant. He was over a year away from convincing the many skeptics in Britain, within the RAF Bomber Command, and in the British Government, including Prime Minister Churchill, that the Americans could match their bravado with results.

British citizens, in and out of the military, were weary. They had been fighting the powerful Luftwaffe virtually alone for over two years, and while they had high hopes that the American bombing would be a key factor in bringing the conflict to an end, many had their doubts. Not even the most optimistic among them believed that the modest beginning would, by the spring of 1944, be transformed into formations of 1,000-plus bombers flying daily missions over key German targets. Then, those that doubted Eaker's early words were glad indeed that the Eighth Air Force came to Britain.

On January 21, 1943, the Combined Chiefs of Staff (CCS), issued what became known as the Casablanca Directive, which stated the objective of the allied air forces as "the progressive destruction and dislocation of the German military, industrial, and economic system, and the undermining of the morale of the German people to a point where their capacity for armed resistance is fatally weakened." Since the destruction of German submarine yards was still vital to the flow of British sea traffic, they were placed at the top of the target priority list, with the German aircraft industry a close second. Transportation, oil, and other targets within the war industry followed in that order.

The CCS did allow room for adjustment of targets as the strategic situation evolved, and on June 10, 1943, RAF Air Marshall Harris, Commander of RAF Bomber Command, and General Eaker received the Pointblank directive that moved the destruction of the German fighter forces to the top of the priority list, and required the two bomber commanders to give aircraft in the air and on the ground, along with the entire manufacturing process, top priority in mission planning.[1]

That meant striking such targets as the Messerschmitt factory at Regensburg, the ball bearing factory at Schweinfurt, and other supporting industries, all beyond the range of fighter escorts and all protected by the best defenses the Germans had to offer, including the Messerschmitt 109 and Focke Wulf-190, each arguably equal to if not better than any fighter in the world.

As Eaker prepared to implement the bomber offensive, he faced not only a serious deficiency in both aircraft and crews and no long range fighters to escort the bombers on deep penetration missions, but also disagreements with Churchill, Harris, and other British officials on whether to continue daylight precision bombing, or accept the British method of conducting missions only at night. Churchill resolved the issue when he reluctantly gave his blessing to daylight precision bombing, with the Eighth Air Force bombing by day and the RAF by night; an operating procedure referred to as "round the clock bombing."

While the debate over nighttime versus daylight bombing would continue between the two air forces for the duration of the air war, and would in fact carry over into the post-war years, no one doubted that daytime bombing, while costly in aircraft and crews, was the best approach to precise destruction of specific targets. To compensate for the lack of accuracy inherent in nighttime bombing, the RAF used radar equipped pathfinder aircraft to find such targets, which meant mixed results over wide areas and inevitable collateral damage to the civilian population. Neither Harris nor other RAF officials voiced concern with the latter damage, and in fact, breaking German morale increased in importance as targets of choice as the air war increased and led to the much-debated and often-criticized devastating bombing of such population centers as Hamburg and Dresden. As early as November 1943, Harris informed Churchill that such attacks could very well bring the war to a close much earlier than predicted, and with the help of the Eighth Air Force and a maximum effort directed at Berlin, "could cost Germany the war."[2]

A further important outcome of daylight, as opposed to nighttime bombing, was the opportunity to draw German fighters into bomber formations, thereby taking a deadly toll on their numbers and seriously impacting the total strength and effectiveness of the Luftwaffe. Therefore, while target accuracy would never be what either the Eighth Air Force or RAF Bomber Commands hoped, destruction of much of the Luftwaffe would. In fact, bomber formations, especially over critical German targets, became "bait" that anxious Luftwaffe pilots willingly took. In doing so they brought down many of the Fortresses and Liberators but, as hoped, with a decided loss to their own fighter force. By mid-1944, the Luftwaffe's tactical fighter strength was so seriously depleted that the allies greatly decreased its ability to support ground operations when it was needed—especially on the beaches of Normandy.

But to prove his strategy, Eaker first had to acquire enough aircraft and crews to match his plans. Both Torch, the North African campaign in the fall of 1942, and Trident, the Italian campaign in the spring of 1943, seriously drained the bomber fleet, as many Eighth Air Force bombers and crews were transferred to the Twelfth and Fifteenth Air Forces. During that same dark period, the training pipeline for crews barely provided enough replacements to fill the personnel gaps in the bomb Groups, and the Eighth Air Force efforts "were essentially experimental." General Eaker could launch approximately one hundred aircraft for any single mission by stretching his crew availability to the maximum. Consequently, airmen joining the bomb groups scarcely had the time to become acquainted with their bases and fellow crewmen, when they were thrust into some of the deadliest bombing missions of the war.[3]

During the uncertain months in the early spring of 1943, as the bombing war really began, Alabamians Howard Abney and Louis Kline were among the early arrivals. In keeping with the Pointblank directive and subsequent interpretation by Eighth Air Force commanders, destruction of the Luftwaffe forced deep penetration missions to targets heavily defended by both fighters and flak, resulting in losses so serious that Spaatz, Eaker and other staff officers and commanders had doubts as to whether or not the Eighth Air Force would survive. Abney and Kline were about to experience firsthand the reasons for such doubts.

In May, Kline reported for duty with the 379th Bomb Group, at Kimbolton, about 15 miles east of Cambridge, as a flight engineer and top turret gunner. A month later Abney joined the 303rd Bomb Group at Molesworth, 10 miles north of Kimbolton, as a tail gunner. At the time, the 303rd had already experienced a heavy turnover of crews and aircraft as a result of numerous losses in early missions from both the accuracy of antiaircraft fire and the deadly efficiency of the German Luftwaffe, thereby acquiring the nickname of "Hell's Angels."

Enemy pilots were flying the highly maneuverable and efficient single engine Me-109, the newly acquired and highly efficient Focke Wulf FW-190, and twin engine Bf-110, among others. In their first briefing the two men were confronted with the somber fact that losses were so bad only one airman out of three could expect to complete his twenty-five missions, the number needed to go home. Anyone completing beyond about six missions was said "to be living on borrowed time." Abney remembered the chilling effect such a dire prediction had on morale. In line with that estimate, of every five airmen who reported to bomb groups during that period, two would not complete their tour due to death, wounds, or becoming prisoners of war.[4]

During the first quarter of 1943, the Eighth Air Force also assisted the RAF in its efforts to destroy German submarine yards, to attempt to stop the deadly toll U-Boats were taking on allied shipping. Admiral Karl Donitz, German U-Boat commander, believed Germany could defeat Britain only by controlling the sea lanes around British waters, and in those early months seemed capable of proving his point.

Fortunately, for the Allies, Hitler refused to allot needed Luftwaffe protection for U-boat operations, and after March, when forty-two submarines were lost, Germany began to lose the battle for control of the Atlantic.[5] To achieve this success, the Eighth Air Force, from January through the first quarter of 1943, concentrated about sixty of its missions on submarine yards assisted by thirty such efforts from the RAF. The figures in the second quarter were fifty-two and thirty respectively.[6]

By May, as the diversion of aircraft to Torch subsided, Eighth Bomber Command had 279 bombers available for missions. The number of available crews began to increase during the same period, and General Eaker was able to put approximately one hundred heavies in the air for a single mission, in four B-17 and two B-24 groups, in addition to the 4th Fighter Group equipped with P-47s and assisted by RAF Spitfires for escort duty. Two more P-47 groups were added in May.

On May 29, Kline received his baptism of fire on just such a mission to the submarine pens at St. Nausari, France. Like many young men, he had falsified his enlistment document, and entered the Air Force at age sixteen. At eighteen, when he took his position in the top turret of the B-17, he was the youngest crew member in the 303rd Bomb Group. Looking back at that mission he admits that he "was really scared, and had he known what was in store for him, he might have been more so, as his squadron got the worst manhandling of his entire career... ." He faced reality head on when several of the 303rd aircraft were knocked from the sky, including the Squadron Commander's bomber. However, when Kline's bomber screeched safely to a halt at Kimbolton, he had a "strange feeling of accomplishment," and actually "felt like a seasoned veteran." In a matter of a few hours he had matured.[7]

Twelve days later, on June 11, Kline flew on the Eighth Air Force's second mission to the submarine yards at Wilhelmshaven, still a deadly target, especially since neither the American nor British fighters could escort the bombers all the way to the target. The air force's *Combat Chronology 1941-1945,* notes that the June 11th mission to Wilhelmshaven clearly demonstrated the difficulty of operating beyond the range of fighter escorts combined with enemy fighter attacks that prevented accurate bombing of the target.[8] Kline readily agrees with that analysis, and remembers that in a formation of 168 Flying Fortresses, the swarm of experienced Luftwaffe fighters gave him a feeling of " indescribable terror and loneliness."[9]

Even a formation of B-17s, with some 1,680 fifty-caliber machine guns and crisscrossing fire from every direction, was far from invincible when the Messerschmitts and Focke Wulf's ripped through the bomber stream. As three ME-109s made repeated passes at 12 o'clock high, Kline remembers his "teeth chattering and his knees knocking at the same time." He recalls that "the tail gunner called off two fighters that were flying abeam of us out of gun range, but they climbed on up for another pass. It seemed that the attacks continued for about an hour and we saw several B-17s drop out of formation, some with smoke trailing. When this happened, the fighters concentrated on the stragglers until they were shot down...

As cold as it was, we in the cockpit and the nose were sweating profusely. Then came the flak." Kline recalls the ominous sight of "black puffs of smoke over the target area" and knew the Germans were trying to get the range with a few practice shots. He said, "the terrible part was that we knew it would be impossible to hit our target unless we flew right through the flak. As we approached the area of smoke it seemed like the puffs followed us right along and we fully expected the next one to move over and get us. Every now and then a puff would appear and it would sound like someone had thrown a handful of pebbles on a tin roof." In a scene repeated so many times by other crews in other places, Kline watched as "a B-17 was hit, straggled out of formation and was immediately assailed by several enemy fighters. We saw four parachutes come from the stricken plane before it exploded," he said. The Eighth lost eight aircraft on the Wilhelmshaven mission, and General Eaker and other officials grew more and more concerned that deeper penetration into Germany, which had to come, without long range fighter protection, would be costly at best and prohibitive at worst. Kline knew only that he had seen the horrors of war first hand—and that was only his second mission. He had twenty-three to go.[10]

In missions flown between June 11 and the first Schweinfurt mission on August 17, the Eighth bombed fifteen targets related to the performance or manufacturing of aircraft, while only three were attacks on submarine facilities. The Luftwaffe was to remain the primary target until mid-1944. Further, with the beginning of "round the clock" bombings, heavy bomber missions were finally on a scale large enough to do significant damage to the enemy, but at a terrible cost.[11]

A decided increase in the strength of the Luftwaffe coincided with the allied efforts to destroy the German aircraft industry. In January 1943, the German air force only kept about 353 of its fighters on the Western front. By midyear, the number increased to 600. The German high command was willing to weaken the Eastern and Mediterranean fronts in order to defend Luftwaffe facilities in the homeland.[12] That meant that the Eighth Air Force faced a daunting task on deep penetration missions. Yet General Arnold and General Spaatz did not stop placing demands on General Eaker for results. While the need for fighter escorts was obvious, the strategy of the war would not wait. The invasion of the continent had to come sooner rather than later and planners could not wait for the increase in fighter range that Eighth Air Force commanders so desperately needed.

Also in mid-1943, transfer of aircraft and crews to the Fifteenth Air Force for both continued support of Torch operations in North Africa and the campaign in Italy kept Eaker scrambling for sufficient heavies to carry out his missions. Between July 2 and August 21, one hundred Eighth Air Force aircraft were transferred to the Fifteenth. This left thirteen groups to continue required missions against German targets. All of this meant that in the months between June 1943 into the early spring of 1944 the Eighth experienced its most costly losses in both aircraft and men.

During those costly months, while the Eighth hurriedly built up its bomber force and trained its crews, heavies were going down almost as fast as they could be replaced. Two days after Wilhelmshaven, 102 Fortresses bombed U-Boat yards at Breman with the loss of four B-17s. On the same day sixty other B-17s bombed the U-Boat yards at Kile and another twenty-two Fortresses, more than one third of the strike force, went down. One group, the 95th, lost ten of its sixteen aircraft. Then on June 25, Kline's Group, the 379th, joined 275 B-17s on missions to Breman and Hamburg. Eighteen Fortresses failed to return. On July 28, as the transfer of Luftwaffe fighters from the Eastern front was completed, Eighth Bomber Command's effort to knock out the aircraft works at Kassel and Ochersleben, the deepest venture into Germany since Wilhelmshaven, cost twenty-two bombers out of a force of 330. Not only were German fighter pilots becoming more skilled at penetrating Eighth Air Force formations, but they were especially effective with the use of rockets.[13]

Even the worst pessimist had not predicted the losses that summer that caused many shocked Eighth Air Force commanders to wonder whether or not earlier British warnings were correct. Perhaps daylight precision bombing was too costly. Testimonies from survivors of that dark period repeat over and over that the requirement that twenty-five missions be flown before rotation home seemed a near impossibility, and even the prediction that they had a one-in-three chance of surviving seemed outdated.

While the Eighth Air Force continued to probe at some targets within Germany, the shortage of aircraft and fighter protection forced it to concentrate, along with the RAF, on targets outside of its borders. Abney completed his orientation and onsite training with the 303rd BG and joined fellow Alabamian Kline in a mission to the submarine marshaling yards at Abbeville, France, followed in the next two weeks by trips to Heroya, Norway, and Hamburg Germany. On one of the probing missions to Hamburg, on July 25, Abney destroyed his first Me-109 from his tail gunner position, but also watched in horror as 19 B-17s went down, mostly from enemy fighters.[14]

In one of the Eighth's most successful missions, on July 24, 167 heavies flew 1,900 miles round trip to bomb the nitrate works at Heroya. The attack was so successful that it disrupted work there for more than three months, while putting unfinished aluminum and magnesium plants permanently out of commission. So, missions in July and August produced mixed results, enough to give Eaker hope that the situation would change once he had the resources in numbers of bombers and crews and in fighter support. In addition to some strategic bombing accuracy on targets such as Heroya, in the 1777 bomber sorties the Eighth flew, it destroyed 326 German fighters. However, the loss of 154 bombers and 1540 men, between July 2 and August 21, did cast a shadow over the successes.[15]

So while the Eighth was taking a deadly toll of enemy aircraft, a fact that would eventually pay off when the powerful Luftwaffe was depleted, and while it was having some success against the targets it attacked, Eaker and other officials were worried as to what would happen when Bomber Command returned to critical deep penetration targets. Fighter escorts, or not, he had no choice but to find out. The defining moment came on August 17, as the Eighth launched attacks into the heart of Germany, to bomb the ball bearing factory at Schweinfurt along with the Messerschmitt factory at Regensburg, both Pointblank targets directly tied to the aircraft industry. In terms of percentage of aircraft lost on a single target, that mission and the subsequent mission in October to Schweinfurt, would be the costliest of the war for the Eighth Air Force. Neither mission would be the successful venture Eaker had hoped, as the Eighth not only failed to prove the concept of daylight precision bombing, but faced the fact that air superiority still belonged to the Luftwaffe.

Still, the believers in strategic bombing were convinced that enough bombers and enough crews to offset losses would be sufficient to get the job done. In one of the most extreme examples of hyperbole, an unnamed staff officer in the Eighth Air Force told a reporter that: "You can afford to lose as many planes and crews as you can replace, provided you get through to the target. If you send 1,000 planes to accomplish your job and your production is 1,000 planes a day, then you can lose 1,000 planes a day, to reach the objective. No one has yet determined the point at which the loss ratio begins to affect the morale of the crews. ...Much more important to morale is knowing that the assignment is carried out, regardless of losses."[16]

While that officer's views may have prevailed at headquarters level, for commanders in the bomb groups the more agonizing question was whether moral could hold up with the mounting losses. How much could eighteen-year-old airmen take? On August 17, 3,760 young men attempted to answer those questions over the two critical targets in the heart of Hitler's "Fortress Europe." They would never forget Schweinfurt and Regensburg, and in years to come, any references to Schweinfurt, especially, would bring painful and glassy stares from Eighth Air Force veterans.

When Kenneth McCaleb, Navigator in the 306th BG, and Kline, and Abney, were aroused from their sleep around 2:00 A.M., they did not realize that they were not only to be a part of the largest bomber raid at that time of the war, but would endure air-to-air combat unparalleled in aerial warfare. When they were briefed that they were flying deep into the very heart of Germany, at least one hundred miles further than any mission to that date, to hit Schweinfurt, a place they had never heard of, they felt both anxiety and apprehension. And like the men in all the groups, the most common emotion was summed up in the word "fear." Throughout East Anglia, other crew members of 276 B-17s from nineteen different bomb groups were briefed on the dual mission.

For McCaleb, Schweinfurt was his ninth mission, and followed a harrowing experience three weeks earlier on July 28, when his group bombed the aircraft factory at Kassel, Germany. Anti-aircraft fire knocked out the two inboard engines forcing his bomber to return to England alone. As his B-17 passed over the white cliffs of Dover, McCaleb gave the pilot a heading to the closest airfield located near Canterbury Cathedral. Unfortunately, the RAF airfield was closed, and before the B-17 could make it to another field it ran out of fuel. The pilot did manage a crash landing in a pasture. The following day McCaleb flew another mission to the submarine marshaling yards at Kiel. There he watched two of the nine aircraft in his squadron go down with twelve men killed and eight becoming prisoners of war, an image he would never forget.[17] As he prepared for the August 17 mission to Schweinfurt, he had no idea what he could expect nor that two months later he would be one of the unlucky few to return to the same target.

Schweinfurt and Regensburg were the types of strategic targets envisioned by air theorists dating back to the 1920s. The concept of "precision bombing" of key industrial targets was directed at just such critical targets. Ball bearings were essential to the operation of most military equipment, and a study by the British Air Staff and Ministry of Economic Warfare had concluded that the ball-bearings industry, and especially Schweinfurt, was a high priority target. It stated that "the concentration of over half of the German ball-bearing supplies in this one place presents an opportunity to strike a decisive blow at the vitals of the German war industry which is not shared or appreciated by any other town or industrial target in Axis Europe." In a misguided effort to motivate apprehensive crews, the study concluded that while such missions would bring heavy losses, "any losses should be accepted in an all-out attack on Schweinfurt."[18]

On the other leg of the dual mission the men flying to Regensburg truly understood the importance of their target. The Me-109 had become the nemesis of any aircraft attempting to penetrate the skies of the Third Reich, and curtailment of its production was critical, not only to the winning of the air war, but a very personal thing for the men who went. Ball bearings and German fighter aircraft: what better targets for a "maximum effort?" What better targets to prove the theory of "daylight strategic bombing" while fulfilling the primary objective of the Pointblank policy? Also, on a more ominous note, what better targets to attract Luftwaffe fighters?

Brig. Gen. Frederick L. Anderson, who was appointed Commander of Eighth Bomber Command when Eaker moved up to overall commander of the Eighth Air Force, forwarded the field orders from Pinetree to the seventeen bomber group commanders on August 16, directing the mission to be flown on August 17, weather permitting. Twelve bomber groups of the First Bombardment Wing, under the command of Brigadier General Robert B. Williams, were to strike the three ball bearing factories at Schweinfurt while the other seven groups under the command of Col. Curtis E. LeMay would bomb Regensburg. The wings were to depart from their bases 15 minutes apart, and their flight to the targets would coincide with diversionary attacks from RAF and other American aircraft; the coordinated effort designed to keep the Luftwaffe so busy that the bombers would be successful. For Kline and Abney, the many details of the mission were not their concern. Their thoughts centered on the other nine men in each of their crews and their responsibility in assuring that with their twin barreled fifty caliber machine guns they could fend off experienced Luftwaffe fighter pilots, thereby assuring successful delivery of bombs on the target and safe return to their English bases. For McCaleb, Schweinfurt was to be mission number nine. The twenty-five missions he needed to go home seemed more and more to be an impossible number, as he glanced at the ribbon stretching across Nazi Germany, where no American bomber had dared to go.

As was so often the case, carefully laid plans were one thing while actual mission accomplishment was something else. Such was the case at Schweinfurt with British weather, especially in East Anglia, a major consideration in mission preparation. While the unpredictable August weather had already caused several missions to be aborted, the seventeenth seemed to offer a window of opportunity, and General Anderson was determined to make the most of it. In addition to the uncertainties of the weather, Anderson had to juggle some of the most complicated details of any mission the Eighth had flown. Timing of departure for the two forces was critical. The mission plan called for the seven groups of the Regensburg force to depart their bases fifteen minutes prior to the twelve groups headed for Schweinfurt, hopefully making it difficult for the Luftwaffe to return to its bases and refuel before intercepting the Schweinfurt force. After bombing its target, the Regensburg force was to head for North Africa. There, it would rearm and depart for England the following day, hitting targets of opportunity on the return trip. Every other bomber in Europe was to launch diversionary raids hoping to draw enemy fighters away from the two task forces.

Four P-47 fighter groups were to escort both forces into Belgium, the limit of their fuel capacity, where the bomber forces would then be on their own. The weather window did not hold. Harry Crosby, Navigator in the 100th Bomb Group, remembers that when he went to the briefing you could see the stars and moon. But after taxiing into position for takeoff, the stars and moon disappeared. In his autobiography he reflected the sentiment of most men headed for Regensburg that day, "God, why is it, I asked, that you let the skies be so clear till briefing time, but when I get up in the air with a thousand aircraft milling around me, you sock in the clouds and let us crash into each other? Maybe You are not on our side?"[19] Instead of the Regensburg force departing at 5:15 a.m., it was delayed an hour and a half until a slight improvement in weather conditions, especially the lifting of fog on the runway, permitted takeoff.

Unfortunately, the task force headed for Schweinfurt was delayed an additional two hours. That delay gave the Luftwaffe ample opportunity to refuel, and in the most concentrated attacks the Eighth had witnessed, hit the Fortresses continually from Belgium to the target and return, resulting in the worst loss of bombers and crewmen of any mission they had flown.

Nor did the Regensburg force fare much better. Diversions had not fooled the Luftwaffe, and while the formation proceeded as planned, it drew out the Messerschmitts and Focke Wulfs in force, and in fierce air-to-air combat left the carcasses of 24 B-17s dotting the landscape before it bombed its target and cleared European skies in route to North Africa.

As planners had feared, by the time the Schweinfurt force waved good-by to its friendly fighter escorts, the Luftwaffe had refueled and was ready to unleash everything it had at the B-17s, as Me-109s and FW-190s decimated the formation all the way to the target and on the return to Belgium, before British Spitfires and American P-47s again provided some protection. All told, sixty B-17s went down in the double strike. Many bunks were empty that night.

Kline, had hoped for a "promised R&R" (rest and recuperation) after his aircraft received severe battle damage on a previous mission on August 16 to Paris. Instead, he awoke the next day to discover that his squadron had been loaned to the 305th Bomb Group, a group that was destined to be hit hard by the enemy fighters. W.F. Craven and J.L. Cate, in the official history, *The Army Air Forces in World War II,* describe the intensity of the Me-109 and FW-190, and even some JU-88 attacks as "intense and continuous, with scarcely one group withdrawn when another took its place."[20] Kline remembers the devastating intensity of his opponents. "The Luftwaffe," he said "unleashed every trick and device in its repertoire attacking from every direction," and "In some instances entire squadrons attacked in 'javelin up' formation, which made evasive action on the part of the bombers extremely difficult." He described the attack as "vicious…We found ourselves under fierce attacks from the time we were just a few miles into France until we left France on the way back. We saw every fighter in the German inventory and several bombers being used as fighters, particularly J-88s, trailing bombs on cables through our formations and dropping them on us from above."[21]

Lt. Col. Bernard Lay, who along with Sy Bartlett coauthored the screenplay for the film *Twelve O'clock High,* flew as an observer with the 100th Bomb Group, and in his official report relates the horrifying scenes of the Me-109s decimating the formation: "Swinging their yellow noses around in a wide U-turn, the twelve-ship squadron of Me-109s came in from twelve and two o'clock in pairs and in fours and the main event was on. A shining silver object sailed past over our right wing. I recognized it as a main exit door. Seconds later a dark object came hurtling through the formation, barely missing several props. It was a man, clasping his knees to his head, revolving like a diver in a triple somersault. I didn't see his chute open."[22]

Many airmen that day were left with the lingering memory that someone could have navigated to Schweinfurt by following the trail of burning bombers and German fighters. The gunners were constantly firing at the enemy, in some cases piling cartridges a foot deep on the aircraft floor. The pilots were busy taking violent evasive action, forcing us to "just spray the sky, hoping to hit something," said Kline. Since the fighters normally came in from twelve o'clock high, Kline was forced to look into the sun. In spite of the difficulties, with experience from eighteen previous missions, he used his skill to destroy one FW-190 while damaging a Me-109.[23]

Abney's group, the 303rd, was among the last to hit the target and consequently had to bomb through immense smoke from previous bomb hits. The best it could do was to drop incendiary bombs in the center of Schweinfurt, hoping for some significant damage. His group's lead bombardier was wounded on the bomb run, requiring the navigator to release the bombs manually with no guarantee that he even came close to the target. Abney, who in eight previous missions had two Me-109s to his credit, increased his kills to three.[24]

Relatively speaking, the lead group, the 306th in which McCaleb navigated, came through the terrible ordeal over Schweinfurt with minor damage and no loss of men or planes. Arriving over the target after the earlier groups had dropped their bombs, McCaleb, like Abney, remembers that his bombardier was unable to see the factories for the smoke caused by the earlier bombing, but his group did drop its bombs in the center of the obscured target area, and while he had no visible evidence was confident that his bomber did inflict damage on the factory. After escaping from the flak over the target, he had to contend again with enemy fighters until his group picked up the protection of fighter escorts. Thankfully, the Luftwaffe did not attack with the ferocity of the trip to Schweinfurt, and no B-17s were lost on the return trip.[25] However for McCaleb, Abney, and Kline, like other airmen, the happiness of their own survival in the worst air battle they had seen was marred by the sight of columns of smoke and wreckages of aircraft below them, and the many empty hard stands greeting them on arrival at their bases. Many men they had seen at breakfast that morning would not be among the lucky ones to return to British soil.

A total of 376 bombers went to Schweinfurt and Regensburg, but only 316 returned to England, the worst loss the Eighth Air Force had suffered as of that date. Another 162 returning B-17s were damaged and a total of 601 men went down with their planes, of which 102 were killed. At the debriefing, crews reported 288 German fighters destroyed. However, as was often the case, reports of enemy losses were probably exaggerated and figures may have been inflated by more than 100 aircraft. As for mission accomplishment, both targets were partially put out of commission, but within a couple of months would again be furnishing Me-109s and ball bearings to the Luftwaffe. Consequently, American and British bombers would need to revisit both factories on several occasions during the war.

Abney's joy at having survived Schweinfurt was short lived. Two days later his group attacked the airdrome at Gilze-Rijen, Holland. It was described by some of the participants as a "milk run," especially compared to the Schweinfurt experience. Such was not the case. Due to haze and flying into the sun, the 303rd Bomb Group was forced to make two passes at the target, placing its bombers in enemy air space for over an hour. By the time it released its bombs, the other groups had already begun their return trip to England escorted by the P-47s. This left the 303rd to bear the brunt of attacks by FW-190s all the way to the Channel. Abney remembers the fighters coming in from every direction. He hit one FW-190 from his tail gun position, but before the fighter went down, the pilot was able to fire a 20mm shell that hit the left horizontal stabilizer and exploded. Abney was knocked unconscious, and when he awoke realized that he was wounded in the right arm and hip. Another crewman, John Doherty, described Abney as "bleeding profusely, and blood all over him." He was one of six men in his group to be wounded, in addition to the twenty-one men who went down in two fortresses. Fourteen other bombers were damaged on that so called "milk run." While Abney increased his total of enemy aircraft destroyed to four when the FW-190 went down, earning him the Distinguished Flying Cross, he had flown his last mission. His crew wrote his wife that they would "miss his trigger finger." After recovery from his wounds, he was assigned to instructor duty. On October 20, his former crew that had survived twenty-three missions, a rare feat in 1943, was shot down on a strike against a factory-railroad center at Duren, to the east of Aachen, Germany. The crew did survive and spent the remainder of the war in a German Stalag.[26]

Klien's luck would hold, and he completed his 25th mission on October 20, the day that Abney's former crew was shot down. Among his missions was the strike at Munster, a major rail center in the Ruhr Valley. Since Munster was not too deep into Germany, P-

47s with auxiliary fuel tanks provided escort duty, thus keeping the enemy fighters away from the formation for a good part of the mission. However, the intensity of flak was some of the worst the crews had experienced. Many crews remember hearing fragments peppering the aircraft like pebbles and the feeling of being sitting ducks. While Klien's Group did survive the ordeal, thirty B-17s were lost in the Munster mission, including twelve out of fourteen in the 100th Bomb Group, a group that more than earned its description as the "bloody 100th."[27]

After twenty-five missions, Klien miraculously returned home without a single injury. He was eighteen, the age when most young people complete high school.[28] For McCaleb, the worst was yet to come. In the two months following Schweinfurt, he survived several horrific experiences, including a mission to Bremen in which his group lost three B-17s. Then came the second week of October and a mission that would even overshadow the Bremen experience. He remembered that "the Group had flown three missions in three days, and the men needed a breather. Monday October 11, we rested—we were tired," he said. "I had only seven more missions to go to complete my tour of twenty-five missions." Then three days later came the mission everyone dreaded—Schweinfurt, again. McCaleb's missions along with his role in the air war would end on number nineteen.[29]

Guy Cofield, 379th Bomb Group, stretcher bearer for wounded B-17 crewmen. (Courtesy: Guy Cofield)

B-17s in route to targets in Germany with contrails of fighter escorts. (Source: National Air & Space Museum)

Parameter Road, Thorpe Abbotts Air Field, home of 100th Bomb Group

B-24 Crew, 466th Bomb Group (Courtesy: Glenn Taylor)

Henry Arnold, Ball Turret Gunner, 94th Bomb Group
(Courtesy: Henry Arnold)

5

Darkness Of Winter, Light Of Spring

We were full of adventure, enthusiasm, confidence, youth, and ignorance.
Roy Davidson, 94^{tth} Bomb Group

One Schweinfurt should have been enough for any man to endure. Kenneth McCaleb felt lucky to have survived the first strike on that crucial ball-bearing factory, and did not care for the odds of going there again. He was right to be concerned.

On October 14, after two days of inclement weather, the skies cleared over Germany, and General Eaker determined to seize the opportunity to return to Schweinfurt again before winter weather would limit flying. Also, the earlier mission in August had not been as successful as either he or his bosses had hoped in stopping production of ball bearings. In fact, since August, the plant complex production was back to sixty percent. Since the German aircraft and vehicles moved on ball bearings, Schweinfurt had to be destroyed, and this time the entire force would strike it and not be split between two targets, as had been the case in August. To many officials in both the RAF and Eighth Air Force, as Schweinfurt went, so went the Luftwaffe. From General Arnold down to the lowest command element, the mission was also to be another test of the concept of daylight precision bombing. Could a maximum effort without fighter escorts penetrate Hitler's Fortress Europe and destroy a key industrial target?

Roy Davidson, a pilot from Birmingham, joined McCaleb and the 94th Bomb Group for the Schweinfurt mission. Davidson had flown four missions since his arrival in August; that included a trip to the well-fortified submarine yards at Bremen, in which his B-17 returned with more than 100 bullet holes. He and his crew had not had a day off since he reported to his group and he was looking forward to a three-day pass that had been approved for October 14. Such was not to be. At 3:30 that morning he was awakened by a flashlight shining in his eyes and a sergeant informing him he was scheduled to fly. "But we are to start a three-day pass today," Davidson said. "Sorry, but a captain wanted to go to London this weekend and you got outranked," he replied. With no idea as to the mission for that day, Davidson shaved, dressed, and headed for breakfast of spam and fresh eggs instead of the usual powered ones, an indication of a bad day ahead. He did not know that he was eating the last "good" meal he would have for the duration of the war.[1]

At 4:30 a.m., Davidson and McCaleb, like pilots throughout East Anglia and the Midlands, headed for the briefing still not knowing what was ahead of them on that Thursday, better known in the years to come as "black Thursday." They waited with the usual nervousness as the briefing officer pulled the map cover back, and when they saw the ribbon stretching deep into Germany, all the way to Schweinfurt, Davidson remembered a "chorus of moans." He had heard some of the horror stories about the first Schweinfurt mission and the fury of the Luftwaffe's stubborn defense of the target, memories he could not shake from his mind. McCaleb needed no reminder! He never forgot the opening remarks from the briefing officer: "Gentlemen, the target for today is Schweinfurt." It would be a long mission, and he could expect to be in the air for nine hours under the best of conditions. He preferred not to think of the alternative.

They were told to expect 1,100 German fighters in route to and from Schweinfurt and some fifty to sixty antiaircraft guns defending the target. The bombers would be protected by P-47s as far as Paris, but after that they would be on their own. Davidson recounts the usual routine as he left the briefing. "Each crew member was given three candy bars and an escape kit which was to be used in case we were shot down in enemy territory. The escape kit contained our picture in civilian clothes and was to be used as phony identification in enemy territory. ...Candy bars were something special. Since leaving the States, we never got them except at mission time." he said. Virtually every officer preparing for a mission shared the common experience of wondering whether or not this was to be his last. Consequently, on every base the briefing was followed by a large number of visits to the Chaplain. Davidson remembered that the number was unusually large after the Schweinfurt briefing.[2]

The plan for the attack called for every available bomber to fly, operating in three bombardment divisions. McCaleb and the 306th Bomb Group would be part of the First Division and would lead the attack entering Germany through northern Belgium, west to Aachen, and then southwest to Schweinfurt. Davidson in the 94th Bomb Group would be part of the Third Bombardment Division that would enter Schweinfurt in a parallel bomber stream approximately thirty miles to the south. It would be accompanied by 196 P-47s until Paris, where fuel limitations would force the fighters to return to England. The Second Bombardment Division would fly a northern diversionary route hoping to attract some of the fighters defending Schweinfurt away from the two attacking divisions.

After taking off in typical English fog Davidson remembers the relief he felt clearing the runway considering the maximum load of bombs and fuel in the bomber, and a runway that was just long enough for takeoff. There was no room for error, and Davidson like every other pilot, had heard horror stories of deadly crashes at the end of runways. The groups made their way through the soupy overcast, exercising extreme caution to avoid collision with other bombers. They cleared the overcast and formed at 21,000 feet where they were joined by the P-47s that were appropriately referred to as "the little friends." Davidson remembers the scene as the P-47s joined the formation: "They were several thousand feet above us. It was a beautiful sight to see the contour trails crisscrossing. To the fishermen below the sight must have been even more spectacular with the four straight vapor trails from each of the 200 bombers and one crisscrossed trail from a large number of fighters."

Just beyond Paris, the bomber crews watched the P-47s reach the limit of their fuel range, turn, and head for home. The last of the escorts was hardly out of sight when the First Division was hit in force by Me-109s, Bf-110s, and FW-190s. Davidson remembers that the radio silence was suddenly broken with the cry over the intercom, "fighters at six o'clock low. Gibson, ball turret gunner, had been the first to spot the Me-109 as it came into range behind us and he began firing from his ball turret as did Mungenast, the tail gunner. Gibson suddenly became ecstatic and was shouting, "I got him, I got him. Look at him go down in smoke! There was more excitement aboard our plane then we ever had been in before," said Davidson. "What fun, what a sport! ...Suddenly it seemed the whole German air force was coming at us from all directions and the air was full of chatter as the radios reported all the approaching fighters, along with a not too infrequent exclamation of joy, as some gunner reported another kill." In reflection in later years, Davidson like so many other young men involved in such excitement, never believed that his B-17 would join the others that were falling out of the sky in such an unbelievable air battle. He said, "we were full of adventure, enthusiasm, confidence, propaganda, youth and ignorance...."[3]

Before the force reached Schweinfurt, twenty-eight B-17s had already gone down. The attacks were especially well coordinated with the use of rockets, large-bore cannons, air-to-air bombing and concentrated punishment directed at certain groups. The German Air Force performance was described by military analysts as "unprecedented in its magnitude, in the cleverness with which it was planned, and in the severity with which it was executed."[4]

Both McCaleb and Davidson survived the trip to the target. There they encountered some of the deadliest flak the Eighth Air Force had seen. "We were sitting ducks," remembers Davidson. "The bombers had to hold a steady straight course and maintain the same altitude in order to align the bomb sights." Then Davidson recalls that the Germans did something unusual. "They sent their fighters after us right through their own flak."[5]

McCaleb's luck ran out on the bomb run when his plane was hit by flak, knocking out three engines. The pilot rang the bailout alarm just before the aircraft went into a flat spin. Along with all of the crew McCaleb successfully bailed out. He broke both legs when he hit the ground. After being unconscious for thirty minutes, he awoke to find himself surrounded by peasants with pitchforks. As bad as he felt, he was relieved when his captors turned him over to the Luftwaffe.[6]

Meanwhile Davidson successfully released his bombs and felt very lucky as he turned west headed for home. For about forty-five minutes the formation was under constant attack from the Me-109's. Then as the fighters ran low on fuel in the vicinity of Mannheim, Mungenast reported from his tail gunner position a Me-110 out of range of his machine guns. "They're shooting something at us that is leaving a black stream of smoke," he reported. What they discovered later to be a rocket exploded about 300 yards behind the bomber. Two more rockets were launched, one exploding a hundred yards behind the bomber without damaging it, but then the other exploded just beneath the plane and lifted the bomber about 200 feet. For the next several minutes, Davidson and his copilot fought desperately to keep the Fortress in the air. "The plane seemed to want to do a loop," he said, "for the flaps had been knocked down as well as the elevator trim tabs by what we later learned was an air-to-air rocket fired by the Me-110. We had never heard of a rocket and had no defense against it."

Then about everything that could go wrong did. The top gunner and engineer, Fred Kruger, reported that the bomber had lost its oxygen, forcing Davidson to take the aircraft down and out of formation. "There appeared to be a cloud cover far below us," he remembered, "and I thought I could fly just above the clouds and if attacked could duck into the clouds and fly on instruments to escape." About thirty minutes later, as he was trying desperately to make contact with the P-47s that were supposed to provide escort back to England, the plane was met by two Me-109s. Davidson continues his account: "Suddenly, the three o'clock fighter turned straight at us and the leading edges of his wings lit up as the 20-mm cannon fired point blank at us. At that moment I must have been the thinnest I'd ever been in my life. I knew the cannon shot was coming straight at me and I sucked in my gut so much that my backbone must have protruded through my belt buckle. At the same time I pulled back on the stick and kicked hard on the right rudder. This headed me straight for the fighter and sharply upward. The Me-109 just barely avoided me as I headed for it, and must have given the pilot a scare also, but somehow the cannon fire did not hit us." After that he remembers both fighters taking turns shooting at his bomber, but fortunately the shots did not connect. When the fighters gave up, Davidson suddenly encountered very heavy anti-aircraft fire. He later discovered that he had flown over the German anti-aircraft school at Epernay, as luck would have it, the only one in France. After clearing the anti-aircraft fire, Stan Chichester, his copilot, gave him the bad news that he had lost another of his engines, leaving only one. Since the big bomber could not possibly stay in the air on one engine, and it was too low to bail out, he had to get the plane on the ground. Chichester spotted a little clearing that turned out to be a cow pasture. After avoiding trees at the edge of the pasture and a herd of cows directly in his path Davidson brought the aircraft to a stop. His wing did kill two cows and he suspected that there would be extra beef on the black market the following day.[7] The events that followed for both McCaleb and Davidson are related in chapter seven.

While the first Schweinfurt mission in August had been terrible in terms of Eighth Air Force losses, the "Black Thursday" mission was worse. In fact, as of that date, more damage was inflicted on the second trip to Schweinfurt than had been done on any mission to a single target, with sixty B-17s lost along with seventeen destroyed and 121 others damaged. While crews reported that they downed 186 German fighters, German records indicated only thirty-eight destroyed and twenty damaged. The exact number is somewhere in between. The 228 bombers that succeeded in bombing the target dropped 395 tons of high explosives and eighty-eight tons of incendiaries on or near the aiming point.

When the statistics on October 14 were tallied with the results of other missions in the second week of that month, the total was 145 bombers lost and 1,450 airmen killed, wounded, or captured. While Air Force commanders labeled the second Schweinfurt mission a success, the later recuperative ability of Germany to recover hardly justified the confidence. In fact, even the destruction and production of Luftwaffe aircraft, a major goal in keeping with the mission priorities, did not happen, as some 800 aircraft were still in the German inventory in the fall of 1943. In reality, as both combatants licked their wounds and prepared for the next round, neither could claim an advantage. Luftwaffe official records during those dark days were probably as accurate as any evaluations prepared by the Eighth Air Force officials when they summarized the relative strengths: "The level of attrition for both Germany's fighter forces as well as the Eighth Air Force during September and October bordered on the point where both were close to losing cohesion and effectiveness as combat forces. In the long run, considering the massive influx of bombers, fighters, and crews already swelling American bases in England, the Eighth held the strategic advantage. It was, of course, difficult for the crews who flew to Schweinfurt to recognize that advantage."[8]

So from any perspective, long-range strategic bombing was becoming costly, especially for the Eighth without long range fighter escorts, so much so that air planners moved away from deep penetration missions for the remainder of 1943. The poor English weather also dictated some slow down in missions flown. During that time commanders had time to replace crews and aircraft while also evaluating past results and reflecting on necessary steps to gain air superiority.[9] In the meantime pressure was mounting from Generals Arnold and Spaatz for results against Hitler's so-called Fortress Europe, especially with the "second front" looming on the horizon. How were the walls to come down? That was the question posed at all levels, in those dark winter months—and the future of the war depended on the answer.

In addition to its lack of long-range fighter escorts and cooperative weather, the Eighth was also restricted in flying activity by the short days with limited daylight. Bomber Command flew when possible, but was forced to concentrate on port facilities, airfields, and industrial facilities, most within range of escorting P-47s, and newly arrived twin-engine P-38s, along with support from RAF Fighter Command. In the meantime the huge American aircraft industry was in full gear and the personnel and aircraft pipelines were pouring men and equipment into England for the great bomber offensive of 1944.

When 1943 gave way to the new year, the Eighth Air Force had flown 171 missions. In its one year of existence, its leaders had learned a great deal about daylight strategic bombing and in doing so had paid a dear price in aircraft and men. But in spite of the difficulties, especially loss of crews and aircraft, members of the Army Air Forces chain of command from Chief of Staff Gen. Hap Arnold down to group commanders who had seen the agony of air combat first hand, had confidence that in time the heavy bomber could be the weapon system the allies needed for victory over Nazi Germany. Several factors encouraged that optimism. First, in February, specially trained crews brought some nighttime capability to the air war with Pathfinder bombers equipped with the new H2S radar system capable of giving a sharper image of the ground. This enabled the Eighth Air Force to continue some bombing operations even in the winter months. Second, some fighter coverage deeper into Western Germany was possible with both the P-47 Thunderbolt and P-38 Lightening fighters equipped with auxiliary wing tanks. But most important, as early as December, a new little friend, the sleek and highly maneuverable P-51 Mustang, was beginning to arrive at American bases and was escorting bombers to and from their targets. With auxiliary wing tanks, the P-51 Mustang, perhaps the best fighter in the world at that stage of the war, could escort bombers to Berlin and beyond. With its Merlin 61 engine, its speed, high-altitude capability and range, the P-51 became the favorite fighter of the fighter pilots, and in the view of many was the pawn needed for air superiority by the Eighth Air Force.[10]

On January 1, an organizational change was approved, and the United States Strategic Air Force (USSTAF) was established to control all activities of the Eighth, Ninth and Fifteenth Air Forces. General Spaatz was appointed overall commander of all air force operations in Europe, while Lt. Gen. Jimmie Doolittle replaced General Eaker as Eighth Air Force Commander. Eaker took command of the Fifteenth Air Force for the continuing war in the Mediterranean, and where feasible, to support the Eighth Air Force in strategic bombing operations. The Ninth Air Force, commanded by Maj. Gen. Lewis H. Brereton, moved to Southern England to support the D-day operations. Later in the spring Maj. Gen. Hoyt S. Vandenberg replaced Brereton. General Spaatz, operating under the command of Air Marshall Sir Charles Portal, British Chief of Air Staff for General Eisenhower, Supreme Allied commander of Allied Forces for Overlord, could move aircraft between the air forces as he saw fit, and was given control of all strategic target selection for American air forces.

On December 23, 1943, General Arnold outlined the priorities of the air war in a message to commanders of the three air forces. He reiterated the Pointblank Directive under which they had operated since mid-1943, and was directed to "destroy the enemy air force wherever you find him, in the air, on the ground, and in the factories." Of course support for Overlord was front and center in all planning as missions resumed in February, and target selections, especially those that could lead to elimination of the production and operation of the Luftwaffe, were critical toward meeting the goal of obtaining air superiority by D-day.

Henry Arnold, 94th Bomb Group, from Enterprise, Alabama, arrived at Bury St. Edmunds in October, and received his baptism of fire on the winter missions of November and December. Due to the distinction of being the smallest man in his crew, Arnold was awarded one of the most dangerous jobs in a B-17, the ball turret gunner. He described the ball turret as "similar to an upside-down top turret...Inside the ball there was something like a curved chair in which you sat in a normal position when the guns were pointed downward, but you would lie on your back while the guns were pointed horizontally." Arnold remembered "spending most of his time in the horizontal position, sometimes for as long as nine hours at a time. When an enemy fighter turned in my direction," he said, "all hell broke loose...You were expected to identify the oncoming fighter; was it a Me-109 or a P-51? An FW-109 or a P-47?...After pushing your mike button, you keep the bastard centered on the cross hairs by moving your left foot and hand controls and firing the twin fifties with your thumb! This all happened within one half to two seconds during which you may fire six to twenty-five rounds from each gun. When there was nothing else to do, you checked your oxygen supply, set the thermostat for the electrically heated suit, pointed your guns down, and opened your hatch and threw spent rounds and gun-clips into the waist. When it was cold, forty to eighty degrees below zero, and humidity went up because of the sweat, ice would form within the oxygen mask requiring you to squeeze the mask to crack the ice."[11]

Such was the case on December 13, 1943, when Arnold, on only his third mission, tested his gunnery skills on a mission to bomb the submarine yards at Kiel. As he squeezed into the ball turret that would be his home for the next seven-and-a-half hours, he was told the cheerful news that six months earlier the 94th Bomb Group hit Kiel and lost nine bombers. Now, the Eighth Air Force was to put 710 heavy bombers in the air, the first mission involving more than 600 aircraft, perhaps a major difference from the earlier mission in which only 400 bombers had been available. Also, the mission was significant in that a few of the long awaited P-51s, together with P-47s and P-38s with added wing tanks, escorted the bombers all the way to the targets. While the 94th Bomb Group struck Kiel, the other groups bombed port areas at Bremen and Hamburg.

Arnold recorded in his diary that about thirty enemy fighters attacked his group for some twenty minutes en route to the target. "The Jerry fighters really gave us hell for a long time," he wrote, "until our own fighter escort P-38s, P-51s, and p-47s got there, then Jerry tamed down quite a bit." During the melee Arnold scored his first victory when he destroyed an ME-110, the only enemy fighter downed on that mission. All nineteen bombers in the 94th Bomb Group returned to their base at Bury St. Edmunds with only minor battle damage.[12]

On January 30, 1944, on his eleventh mission, Arnold was part of the resumption of deep penetration missions when 701 bombers with fighter escorts bombed the industrial area around Brunswick. "We had wonderful fighter support all of the time," he wrote, and though twenty bombers were lost, the story would have been much worse on such a mission two months earlier.[13] In addition to the fighter escorts, the Eighth Air Force finally had a sufficient number of bombers and crews to carry out the type of strategic bombing operations General Arnold had requested.

While weather had been a factor in hampering operations through January, on the second week of February, conditions began to change, and from February 20 to 25 breaks in the murky overcast created flying conditions for the "Big Week." Together with RAF Bomber Command, the Eighth Air Force bombed five factories related to the manufacture of aircraft during that week. Those missions were some of the most critical of the air war, and significantly reversed the war against the Luftwaffe that to that point had not gone well. Following that week, the Luftwaffe took on a strictly defensive role and most importantly would not be a major factor in defense against Overlord. However, as General Doolittle stated, "We paid a price for the air." During the Big Week alone the Eighth Air Force lost 344 bombers, 33 fighters and 2,473 men.

The week began with one of the Eighth's most spectacular successes: the combined attack on the Messerschmitt assembly plants at Bernberg and Leipzig. For the first time more than 1,000 B-17s participated, and followed RAF bombing that had occurred the previous night. As was often the case night bombing by the RAF served to alert the enemy to the likelihood of an American raid the next day. And so it was on February 20. The Luftwaffe was ready and hit the bomber formation in force placing some of the Fortresses under constant attack for three hours. Twenty-one bombers were lost on that first day portending a difficult and costly week.

After standing down for most of February due to poor weather, William (Bill) Lawley, B-17 pilot in the 305th Bomb Group, was awakened at the usual 2:00 a.m. and told that he would fly. Following a breakfast of eggs and spam, the briefing officer pulled the cover from the map and the tape reached deep into Germany to the ME-109 assembly factory at Leipzig. Past missions directed at aircraft assembly plants, such as efforts to knock out the ME-109 factory at Regensburg, left little doubt that the mission, Lawley's ninth, was to be a rough one. He remembered that the weather was absolutely perfect, with the British skies "bluer than he'd ever seen them." He departed about daybreak and joined the formation of three six-ship elements on the squadron leader's right wing. Except for encountering some flak the flight to the target was routine. Then, as the B-17 reached the target, and the bombardier attempted to release the bombs, he discovered that they were hung up. When he could not release the bomb load, Lawley had no choice but to fall out of formation, where he was greeted by approximately 20 FW-190s and

Me-109s, upholding the sometimes used metaphor of "wolf pack," swarmed over the bomber, attacking from the front and rear.

On the first pass, a 20mm shell burst through the copilot's windshield. The copilot, who was killed instantly, slumped over the control column and forced the bomber into a steep descent. "I think we went into a spiral, not a spin," Lawley recalled. "We were at 28,000 feet, and we went down to 12,000. I finally got it leveled off at that point." Lawley, seriously wounded himself and bleeding profusely, recalls the difficulty he had of flying the aircraft with an instrument panel and windshield covered with the blood of the dead copilot. By looking out his left window and using the horizon to maintain his bearing, and with the help of his bombardier who had some previous pilot training, he regained some control of the aircraft. Then he realized the seriousness of his situation. His instruments were no longer functioning, one engine was on fire, and he had no forward visibility. Therefore, he ordered the crew to bail out. After one crewman exited the bomber, his bombardier informed him that eight crew members were wounded and two could not bail out. Lawley then had no choice but to nurse the bomber back to England. As he neared the French coast, a burst of flak set another engine on fire and the fully loaded bomber began to lose altitude rapidly. After almost passing out due to loss of blood, and with one engine out, another on fire, and then having to feather still another, Lawley fought desperately to maintain his altitude.

Just as it appeared that he would crash into the channel, he attempted one more time to jettison the bombs. That time he succeeded, thereby decreasing the rate of descent. Then as the lightened bomber descended to 1,000 feet the English coast came into view. As he barely urged the plane over the white cliffs of Dover, he spotted a fighter base landing strip and brought the crippled plane in for a belly landing. He had landed at "Red Hill," a Canadian base about fifty miles south of London. All of the wounded airmen that he refused to abandon survived. Six months later, on August 8, Lawley was ordered to General Spaatz's headquarters where he was presented the Medal of Honor. After returning to his home base at Chevelston, in keeping with policies concerning Medal of Honor recipients, he received orders returning him to the States.[14]

Henry Arnold also saw plenty of action in the Big Week and really became acquainted with his ball turret position. On February 24, his group was scheduled to bomb an airfield at Tutow, but due to weather conditions there, they were forced to hit the secondary target at Rostov. In his diary he recorded his frustration with the enemy fighters that mostly stayed out of range of his fifty-caliber machine guns but within range of their rockets, some coming dangerously close to his bomber. "We didn't have any fighter escorts at all," he said, "and the enemy fighters gave us hell for three hours. It was very uncomfortable to see the rockets burst in our formation and know that we couldn't shoot back at them because they were out of our range." Fortunately, no bombers were lost, in spite of the repeated rocket attacks.

The following day Arnold was awakened at 3:45 a.m. and told that he was going to Regensburg to bomb the ME-109 factory, a target that had caused so many casualties on the Regensburg-Schweinfurt mission the previous August. Unlike the August mission, this time the 94th Bomb Group was escorted all the way to the target by P-51 and P-38 fighters with auxiliary wing tanks. Flak became the major problem, and his aircraft returned to Bury St. Edmunds with many flak holes. When he successfully completed that mission, Arnold recalled he had only eight missions to go and was "very grateful that he had successfully returned from so many hazardous trips."[15] However, he did not realize that his worst mission was yet to come.

On March 6, the Eighth launched the first of several missions to Berlin, the German capital, a long-awaited but much-dreaded target. The historic mission mixed all of the excitement and horror they could ask for; excitement of finally hitting the heart of Hitler's Third Reich, and horror at the cost in aircraft and men. Indeed, it was to be the costliest mission of the war in terms of the total number of planes lost. With the exception of 31 B-17s bombing an area southwest of Berlin on March 4, weather had prevented a large scale attack on the capital. When the heavy overcast finally broke, a maximum effort was launched as 730 heavy bombers with 800 fighter escorts hit the metropolitan area of Berlin and nearby cities of Potsdam, Wittenberg, Templin, Oranienburg, and Kalkberg. The bomber stream blackened the sky about ninety miles long, as the huge armada left Dover behind and crossed the English Channel, penetrating enemy air space some 500 miles into the heart of the Third Reich. Air Marshall Hermann Goering had assured the German people that no allied planes would ever appear over Berlin, a promise that rang hollow as they looked at the bomber contrails stretching as far as they could see. But, even though the bombers had the protection of the fighter escorts, the Luftwaffe found holes in the air cover. The significance of the target in the heart of the homeland caused the Luftwaffe to come out in full force with every offensive maneuver they knew resulting in enemy squadrons decimating entire bomber groups.

Arnold awakened at 3:15 a.m., not realizing that he was about to experience the most frightening time he would ever endure. "Breakfast: 0400; briefing: 0500; take off: 0800; return to Bury St Edmunds: 1630; mission duration: 8:30, Position #3, Lead Squadron, ship #540." So his diary read. "It was a living hell," he later recorded. He recalls that the twin scourges of skilled Luftwaffe pilots and deadly flak tore the formation apart, especially in those areas not covered by the fighter escorts. Fortunately, his group did have excellent fighter support, and only lost one bomber. "Our formation was very good," he said, "but the Jerry fighters were determined and we could see B-24s and B-17s blowing up all over the sky…The tail gunner reported eight ships going down from the group behind us…I saw about six or seven ships blow up in groups behind us in less than five minutes. It was an indescribable scene and I have never seen anything like it in any of the raids before this one. I hoped and prayed that we would never go back there. It sure scared the hell out of me."[16]

The 94th Bomb Group was lucky compared to several others. Red Harper, pilot in the 100th Bomb Group, remembered the mission very well. His group was part of the bomber stream the fighter escorts could not cover. With a relatively new crew his aircraft was assigned the number nine position, high squadron, a spot referred to as "tail-end-Charlie." He described it as "the equivalent of being at the end of the line playing pop-the-whip." "Whenever the formation turned," he said "you stall out trying to slow enough to keep from overrunning the formation." But what scared him the most in the rear position was that he "had the dubious honor of being the first target for the hungry Luftwaffe pilots."

And so it was that as the formation penetrated deep into Germany, the German ground controllers discovered a gap in the fighter protection that happened to include the 100th and 95th Bomb Groups. A large force of fighters was scrambled to confront the formation. Harper remembers that "At 11:59 all hell broke loose, and we were attacked by more than a hundred German fighter planes...made up of Me-109s and FW-190s. They hit us head on in pairs. On the first pass, they had six of our nine ship high squadron on fire but missed me. They swung around and came at us again head on and took out two more of our high squadron. They then took out seven more bombers from the lead and low squadrons, making a total of fifteen bombers shot down from the 100th Bomb Group in less than ten minutes. It looked like a parachute invasion," he recalled. "Bombers and fighters were on fire and exploding all over the sky...The Berlin area was filled with the flaming wrecked planes...I saw German pilots firing on American pilots dangling from their parachutes."

Harper suddenly realized that his plane was the only one remaining in the high squadron. When the enemy fighters made another pass, one of his gunners shot down two Me-109s. Then a rocket penetrated the right waist section near the tail and damaged the right stabilizer and some of the bracing. Harper continues, "the rear oxygen tanks were shot out and an electrical cable was severed. We had no choice but to go down and get some air." After what was described in the 100th bomb group history as a "daring dive" down to 5,000 feet, Harper and his copilot managed to find some cloud cover. Flying on instruments and avoiding flak which seemed to follow him across Germany and France, he successfully evaded the fate of the rest of his squadron and limped onto his base at Thorpe Abbotts. Harper was no longer the "new guy" at his base. He was a seasoned veteran, and in his Group, which had appropriately been labeled the "bloody 100th", he was a survivor, no mean feat in March 1944.[17]

The scenes at the various air fields throughout East Anglia were similar as the bomber force returned. On every control tower anxious eyes were fixed on the horizon looking for the dots of incoming bombers, and wondering how many would return. Some bomber groups returned intact while others were broken and piecemeal, with gaps in their formations and red flares indicating wounded aboard.

As the 100th Bomb Group approached Thorpe Abbotts, the sight of what was left of the thirty-six aircraft that took off that morning was sickening to the maintenance crews and base officials counting the returning bombers. Harry Crosby describes the scene in his book *A Wing and a Prayer*:

> "Back at the base, the 100th is hearing that our formation is in trouble. At return time, duty stops and all workers look upward.
> The sound. It is wrong. Engines missing, engines racing too fast. Pilots are having to work their remaining engines too hard.
> Then the formation. One, two, three. The plane that has taken over the lead is missing the whole trailing edge of its starboard wing. Four. Two engines missing. Red-flares, injured aboard. Five, six, seven. Two engines out, one of them ripped completely off the wing. How on earth do those forts stay in the air? Eight. Nine. Ten. That poor bastard of a pilot with his whole left elevator missing is still trying to keep formation. Ragged. Eleven. Twelve. Is that all? No. Here comes three more. Or rather parts of three more. One of them has a hole clear through the fuselage. Red-flares from every plane. Fifteen planes. No more. Missing: half of what went out."[18]

Sixty-nine bombers, 690 men, went down on that historic mission with fifteen belonging to the 100th Bomb Group. Of the returning bombers, 349 were damaged. However, the losses, while the largest number of any mission, were less than ten percent and, to Eighth Air Force officials, that was acceptable. Eleven escort fighters also were shot down. Bomber crews claimed ninety-seven fighters destroyed while the escorting fighters claimed eighty-two. While many bombs fell in the Berlin area, few actually hit the industrial targets.

The mission was declared a qualified success, in that the formation did bomb Berlin, and did take a heavy toll on Luftwaffe aircraft. In fact, the March 6 bombing of Berlin may have been the high water mark for the German Air Force. But, like so many other bombing missions in the war, success was a relative term. For airmen who put their lives on the line, it was still a question of how many missions did they have to complete to go home? On an even more morbid note, whose bunk in the living quarters would be emptied next?

6

Air Superiority

It was very eerie seeing all that metal ripping apart only yards apart, but without a sound as in a movie.

John Hard, 100th Bomb Group

On June 6, 1944, the *Birmingham News* summed up the comments of an anxious people reacting to the day they hoped would be the beginning of the end:

"For a mother on Southside, a father in Pratt City, a sweetheart somewhere in Norwood—for all the numberless wives and children and human persons with love in their hearts for someone in uniform—for all of these, D-Day brought waiting and pain.

At early morning, the workmen catching ACIPCO and North Birmingham and the East Lake buses, the women in slacks with their hair held close in turbans, the traveling men catching an early breakfast before starting out on a mission—they all knew the invasion was on.

One of the first persons to enter Third Presbyterian Church …when radios were blasting the news…was a Negro Sergeant. He stood before the pulpit and told the Rev. James Cantrell, the pastor that he wished to pray silently. The Rev. Mr. Cantrell welcomed him as he did all others who entered the church that day.

...'We'll lick the Germans in 30 days,' a taxi driver said as he speeds toward town.'"

Not since December 7, 1941, had news so captivated the American people. The information flashed into newspaper offices across the nation before midnight, June 6, with final confirmation before daybreak the following morning. *The Birmingham News* headline was typical of what greeted early risers. It read: ALLIES DRIVE INLAND ON WIDE FRONT AFTER INVADING FRANCE, and below the headline, "11,000 Planes Sent Into Skies to Cover Landing of Troops."[1]

Meanwhile, a continent and an ocean away in England, the thousands of men involved in air support for the landing experienced their own anxiety mixed with feelings of relief that the day for which they had been planning during the previous year had finally arrived. From March until June 6, 1944, the Eighth Air Force along with RAF Bomber Command and the Ninth and Fifteenth Air Forces concentrated on targets to support Overlord. While control of the air through destruction of the Luftwaffe led the mission priority list in March and April, and continued to be important until D-Day, transportation targets along the entire Normandy coast with oil a close second, became the primary focus of all air operations. The Allies arrived at those priorities after a great deal of discussion and much controversy, especially between RAF Air Chief Marshall Sir Trafford Leigh-Mallory, with responsibility for tactical air support of the invasion, and bomber commanders General Carl Spaatz and RAF Air Chief Marshall Arthur Tedder. Eisenhower approved the concentration on transportation targets on April 14, with the understanding that after D-Day oil targets would receive top priority.[2]

As it turned out, efforts to destroy transportation and oil targets complemented each other, and with Eighth Air Force bomber and fighter groups at peak strength, the war of so called "imposed attrition" against the Luftwaffe also continued. Consequently, attacks on seventy-five selected railway targets brought German rail traffic in France and Belgium to a complete halt, while reducing oil production by fifty percent, and seriously reducing Luftwaffe capability. Add to those results attacks on oil facilities in the two weeks after June 6, and Germany lost ninety percent of its aviation fuel. While many of the oil facilities would be repaired, follow-up attacks would continue to cripple German oil production.[3]

On May 25, Lawson Corley, bombardier in the 446th Bomb Group, flew one such mission that turned out to be his last. It was his nineteenth, and along with eighty-five other bombers, he was to bomb the rail marshaling yard in the town of Mulhouse, France. Following the mission, he and his crew were to be due for a long awaited seven-day pass. He also looked forward to his assignment as the lead bombardier on D-Day.

Like so many other missions to France, crews looked at it as routine, or "one of the easy ones." And so it was for Corley and his crew, but the return trip to England was another story. Somewhere over Luxembourg, Corley's pilot, Eugene Winn, was forced to feather one of the left props and drop out of formation. Then, as the Liberator neared Brussels it was greeted by intense flak that knocked out two more engines leaving the aircraft with one quarter of its power. Since the bomber could not possibly make it back across the Channel, Winn ordered the crew to bail out. Then, Corley realized his worst nightmare when he noticed flak holes in his chute. But he had no choice but to jump and could only pray that the chute would open. Fortunately, while the chute did hang up briefly as he hurtled through the air, it finally opened, but dangerously close to the ground. The hard landing knocked him out for a few minutes, cracked two vertebrae, ruptured his right kidney, and damaged his spleen. Other crew members landing close by thought he was dead. Then as he regained consciousness, his flight engineer, Walter Niespodziewany, attended to his injury and dragged him into the woods. There, they were met by members of the Belgium underground, who instructed them to remain in the woods while they went into a nearby town, promising to return later that afternoon with food and civilian clothes. Unfortunately the German field police with the help of bloodhounds, found them first. After rough interrogation Corley was sent to Stalag Luft III, where he remained for the duration of the war.[4]

In the month preceding Overlord the Eighth Air Force committed 4,000 bombers in forty bomber groups and fifteen fighter groups to the allied effort. The Ninth Air Force, specifically established to support D-Day, contributed an additional 4,000 bombers and fighters in addition to 1,300 troop carrier aircraft and more than a hundred gliders. While no significant air battles were fought, either before or during the D-Day landings, the two air forces, together with RAF Bomber Command, attacked any possible landing sites including transportation facilities, suspected troop concentrations, anti-aircraft and machine gun emplacements, airdromes, and any other targets that might in any way contribute to German defenses. John C. Butler, engineer and gunner, 453rd Bomb Group, remembers saturating the landing beaches with 100 pound bombs to create foxholes for landing troops.

When D-Day finally arrived, 1,083 B-17s and B-24s from three Eighth Air Force divisions departed their bases in England in waves with instructions to cease bombing no later than ten minutes before the landings. The Ninth Air Force followed between 6:05 and 6:24, attacking coastal batteries and transportation targets, primarily on the Cherbourg Peninsula. Fighters from both air forces provided air cover for the landing forces. Thanks to Luftwaffe attrition in the previous months, only three FW-190s attempted to interfere with the invasion forces. In later testimony German prisoners testified that Allied bombing in support of D-Day was worse than anything they had experienced on the eastern front. But perhaps the most telling statement came from General Eisenhower when he was reported to have stated to an allied officer that "if you see any aircraft they are ours."

Eisenhower was also convinced that without air superiority the invasion may not have succeeded.[5] Lieutenant John Eisenhower, the General's son, graduated from West Point on D-Day, and a week later joined his father on a tour of the Normandy beachhead. He was astonished to see vehicles moving bumper to bumper, in violation of procedures he had learned at West Point. "'You'd never get away with this if you didn't have air supremacy,' he remarked to his father. "The supreme commander snorted, 'if I didn't have air supremacy I wouldn't be here.'"[6]

Most Eighth Air Force crews supporting the landings recall their surprise and relief at the lack of opposition by both the Luftwaffe and anti-aircraft flak on that first day. Glenn E. Taylor, an engineer and gunner in the 466th Bomb Group, said that "the fear he had anticipated for D-Day was worse than the reality of the actual participation. Our briefing officer had assured us that the Luftwaffe would be there in force to meet us... just being afraid would hardly describe it. We were scared to death." Ben White, copilot in the 94th Bomb Group agreed, and credits the lack of opposition to the 32,000 tons of bombs dropped on anti-aircraft gun batteries in the week preceding the invasion. James Smith, B-17 gunner, 94th Bomb Group, referred to the air operation associated with D-Day as "a piece of cake."[7]

Howard Polin was a weather briefer in the 352nd Fighter Group, located at Bodney Airdrome, a British base near Cambridge. On June 5 he knew that the invasion was imminent when he observed the increased security around his base and the sound of putt-putts (portable generators) all night long. He discovered the next day that they were painting black and white stripes on the forty P-51 mustangs to identify them as allied aircraft.

Polin recalls the sights and sounds of P-51s departing for Normandy. "Our Mustangs started take off about the same time," he said, "They took off down the dirt runway, four abreast. Unfortunately one fighter crashed into a new control tower that had just been constructed. The pilot was killed instantly, and for a moment it appeared that the accident could cause a delay. However, delays on that particular day were not permitted under any circumstances. The Group Commander simply ordered the wreckage removed, and the other fighters proceeded without delay."[8]

Taylor describes the enormity of the invasion force as seen from the air: "As we departed the southern coast of England at 'Salsy Bill,' we began noticing the rear echelon of landing craft. The time, perhaps, was a little before 6:00 a.m. on June 6, and we still had the length of the lower Channel to cross. Literally thousands of landing craft cleaved the water 20,000 feet below us. All symmetrical, all in line, all heading east to Omaha, Utah, Sword, or Juno....Moreover, as far as the eye could see: Airplanes! A thousand in front of our group and as many behind." Taylor was fortunate in that as engineer on a B-24 he sat in the nose turret. He said that even with the heavy cloud cover he had "a teasing view of the greatest armada ever assembled in the history of mankind, I was struck by the sudden thought I was witnessing the greatest spectacle yet devised by the human mind." After the mission he received a letter from his father asking if he got to see the "Big Show?" His reply: "Yes, I saw the Big Show," and in later years, reflecting back more than six decades, he says "it's still the biggest one I have ever seen!"[9]

Tom Winslett, B-24 pilot in the 448th Bomb Group, said that "without a doubt D-Day was his most memorable mission. The scene on the beach is as clear in my mind today as it was in 1944." He remembers "boats scattered and twisting in the bay…with guns still firing." He too was relieved that the predicted opposition from the Luftwaffe did not materialize. Even so, he was so anxious to get back to England that he broke formation. "The home base never looked so good," he said.[10]

Aircraft were in the air constantly throughout the day. Taylor flew three missions himself while some of the fighter groups flew many more. Among targets hit by his group were pill boxes on the invasion coast and highway, and other rail targets on key transportation routes into the invasion zone. Polin remembers "P-51s landing and departing Bodney Airdrome continually with pilots coming in only to refuel, snack, and perhaps have a few moments' rest.[11] While the airmen were relieved at the lack of resistance on D-Day, they did not know that the Luftwaffe and the German ground to air defenses were still very much intact, and the air war after D-Day was to be every bit as deadly as before.

Eighth and Ninth Air Force bombers and fighters destroyed virtually every bridge and transportation route during the sixty days before D-Day through June 13. The Eighth Air Force alone launched 6,207 bombers and dropped 16,567 tons of bombs at a cost of 13 B-17s and 14 B-24s a relatively small number when compared to the numbers it lost in the early spring of 1944. Eighth Air Force Fighter Command flew 9,006 sorties during that week in critical tactical support of ground operations with a loss of 135 aircraft.

Within thirty-six hours of the invasion. 200 German fighter aircraft arrived at French airfields, followed by an additional hundred on June 10. Others followed over the weeks that followed, and literally stripped the Reich's fighter defenses, a loss that would be welcomed when bomber operations resumed over Germany. Ultra intercepts picked up most of the arrivals and enabled Allied fighters to keep track of Luftwaffe fighters resulting in heavy losses against the Allied fighters. The Luftwaffe lost another 232 in the second week. A German Major in the 77th Infantry Division, captured at SC Sauvern on June 16, told a fellow prisoner that the Luftwaffe lost sixty-eight aircraft in the first week of operations around the beachhead, and 362 more went down in the next few weeks. Nor was the long term outlook very promising. He said:

"I once [remarked] that the *Fuhrer* said that if the invasion came, he would send the whole G.A.F. [German Air Force] into action at the place of invasion, even if it meant leaving all forces in all other theaters without cover. That story is over as far as I was concerned after I had seen one single German reconnaissance aircraft in the air between the 6th and the 16th, and apart from that, complete mastery of the air by the Americans. We can bring out whole armies, and they'll smash them completely with their forces within a week. Above all, we have no petrol at all left. We can no longer move any numbers of troops by means requiring petrol, only by rail or marching on foot."[12]

Following the successful landings on Normandy, and the commitment of most of the bomber force to close ground support, General Spaatz, and Air Marshall Harris, were anxious to resume attacks on strategic targets as soon as feasible. On June 10, Spaatz developed a plan defining the priorities of a renewed strategic campaign as oil production, the ball bearing industry, tank production, the ordnance depots, and the motor transport industry. General Eisenhower agreed with Spaatz that the resumption of attacks on strategic targets was essential and, except for emergency uses of bombers in tactical situations, permitted him to resume such bombardment as he saw fit.[13]

On June 12, another priority target was added to the list, as the first V-1 "flying bombs" were launched against London. The V-1 was a pilotless, pulse-jet-powered aircraft that flew on a preset compass course until fuel was exhausted and the engine shut down usually somewhere over Southern England. Since it hit targets indiscriminately, it often dropped on population centers, causing many nervous moments in a population that had already endured the horrors of some eight months of nightly bombing during the blitz. On June 15, the Germans began an intensified V-1 attack on allied targets, especially London. More than 300 were launched and 73 actually struck war weary London. Over the month that followed 2,667 were launched, and in spite of intensive efforts by the Eighth, Fifteenth, and Ninth Air Forces, together with the Royal Air Force to intercept the V-1s, the deadly and highly unpredictable weapons continued to terrorize the British people. By March 29, 1945, the day the last V-1 hit London, 6,725 had been launched. Of that number, 3,900 were destroyed by aircraft, anti-aircraft fire, or balloons. The 2,825 flying bombs that fell on England destroyed 23,000 houses and killed 5,500 civilians.

While the V-1 was certainly a terror weapon in the true sense of the word, it was followed by the even more powerful V-2 rocket powered ballistic missile. The V-2 had a trajectory of 60 miles high and 189 miles long, a range sufficient to reach targets throughout England. Also, some were launched at targets on the continent. Although approximately 6,000 were built, many by slave labor, Hitler's efforts to use such weapons, while damaging to British morale, were too little, too late. Even greater numbers would have had little effect on the outcome of the war, and that could only have been changed if the weapons had been armed with atomic warheads. In reality, they merely drained resources and funds away from other more badly needed projects.[14] While V-1 and V-2 facilities were of concern to Spaatz they were third on his target list behind oil and the German Air Force, both considered critical to bringing the war to a close.

Unfortunately, from June 9 to June 17, the weather again became a limiting factor forcing most missions to concentrate on secondary or even tertiary targets. On June 18, it cleared and permitted a maximum effort as 1,239 heavy bombers attacked oil refineries at Oslebshausen and Merseburg, Germany, in addition to a direct and deadly attack on the city of Hamburg. Eleven heavy bombers were lost to anti-aircraft fire.[15]

During that busy period the Eighth Air Force experienced some of the most intense combat it had known. Not only was the Luftwaffe very much alive, but as the Eighth attempted to destroy targets critical to the German war effort, flak became an even bigger factor.

Ben White and William E. Massey, pilots in the 401st Bomb Group, flew several of the post D-day missions and both agreed that flak was heavy and accurate. Such was the case on June 19 when the two men, flying in different groups, bombed the oil refineries at Bordeaux, Merignac, and Landes de Bessac, France. While the trip to the targets was uneventful, flak over the target was intense and Massey, on his nineteenth mission nearly lost his life over Bordeaux. He had just entered the target area at 26,000 feet when his B-17 was hit by flak several times but without major damage. Then it happened. A piece of flak entered the plane and hit the oxygen bottles causing them to blow up and catch fire. Massey ordered the crew to bail out. Suddenly the bomber exploded and he found himself falling through the air, the chute he had been about to snap on miraculously clutched in his hand. After making several attempts to snap the chute on while tumbling through the air, he finally succeeded in buckling it into his harness and pulled the ripcord. It opened at the last minute and landed him in a field of cattle. "I will never forget the jolt that slowed me down," he said, "my boots kept going, so I hit the ground in my stocking feet."

Only Massey and two of his crewmen, his bombardier, Lewis V. Stelljes, and waist gunner, Francis L. Beard, survived the ordeal. They hid for several hours until they were discovered by the French underground. For more than two months he lived with the underground and even assisted in raids on German warehouses and railroads. After seventy-six days, Massey left his hiding place and worked his way past the retreating German lines until he met up with General Patch's army. From there he was flown to England, where he had been declared missing, and later to the States. In the *History of the 401st Bomb Group,* Massey and the two other crew members were recognized as the only three airmen to escape when explosions blew them out of their bombers.[16]

White cannot compare his experiences with those of Massey, but has a vivid recollection of the June 19 mission when 1,257 bombers bombed key strategic targets in Germany, including the Magdeburg oil refinery. He recalls that the flak was extremely heavy and accurate with the 94th Bomb Group sustaining battle damage to fifteen of its eighteen planes. A total of fifty bombers were lost that day, with twenty-one making forced landings in neutral Switzerland.

White felt very lucky that his bomber sustained only minor damage. He does remember that the concussion from the flak was so violent that he had difficulty holding the plane in formation.

The following day White received the dreaded news that once again Berlin was the target. He describes the day as follows: "We took off about 5:00 a.m. loaded with 6,000 lbs. of incendiary bombs. All went well until we got near Berlin where we could see a black cloud of smoke from previous flak bursts above the target area. As we started the bomb run, the flak was intense and our plane shook and bounced. Shortly thereafter our lead plane, with Lt. Col. O'Connor, our Squadron Commander aboard, took a direct hit and went down with no survivors." Again his bomber was hit, but again it stayed in the air. While his luck held, such was not the case for forty-three of the 1,300 that went down on the mission. Many of the other bombers that survived returned with wounded airmen aboard. One B-17 went down with a crewman dangling below his parachute that was caught in the bomb bay mechanism. "The sky was spotted with descending parachutes—images that were forever embedded in the memories of survivors."[17]

In spite of such massive raids, efforts to eliminate oil reserves were not as successful as hoped. So, while the land invasion armies were moving east after breaking through German resistance in France, the efforts to destroy oil intensified. At the same time Hitler was proving his resilience, and crews joining the bomber offensive in the summer and fall of 1944 witnessed combat every bit as fierce as those before them. They also arrived at a time when crews were greeted with the news that the total missions required for rotations home was increased from twenty-five to thirty. Then in the fall the number went to thirty-five. Oil-chemical complexes continued to receive highest priority with many appearing a dozen times on some crew target lists. They included Berman, Hamburg, Magdeburg, Lutzkendorf, Politz, Ruhland, Wesseling, Dusseldorf, Scholven, and Merseburg-Leuna, Germany. The Merseburg-Leuna synthetic oil site was especially resilient, with missions flown there every month, and six in November alone.

Walter H. Fleming, B-17 flight engineer and Gunner in the 487th Bomb Group, especially remembers the November 30 mission there for two reasons. First, it was his last mission. Second, it was his worst. While he had already witnessed the tenacious defense around other targets, the anti aircraft fire around that synthetic oil target was as bad as any he experienced. Twenty-nine heavy bombers went down that day, and sadly, he knew many of the crews.[18] Raymond Hill of Gadsden, Alabama, a B-17 gunner in the 305th Bomb Group, flew five different missions to that elusive target, between August 24 and December 12. He recalls that he wondered why the "heavy chorus of moans" interrupted the August briefing, and by the time he flew his fifth mission to the same target in December, he understood the reason. And, Like Fleming, he lost many friends attempting to destroy German oil.[19]

Frank Bolen had been classified 4-F in early 1942, due to an organ dysfunction called *situs inversus*. But, in September 1942, he attempted again to enlist, and since the disease was not debilitating and because airmen were so badly needed, he was accepted. He became a bombardier and was assigned to the 91st Bomb Group at Bassingbourn. On September 8, 1944, after fifteen grueling missions, he joined the oil campaign. His bomber departed Bassingbourn at 6:00 a.m. to rendezvous with the formation of 950 other bombers that would bomb several targets that day. His group was to bomb the I.G. Farben chemical-oil plant at Ludwigshafen, Germany. He remembers, "I felt more relaxed…on this mission than on any previous fifteen I had flown." As the formation neared the target at 25,000 feet, he remembers flak ahead bursting at the exact altitude he was flying. However he had little time to think about it as he prepared to release the 500-pound demolition bombs. "I bent over the bomb sight, expecting any time to see the chemical plant come into view," he remembers. "Just as I lifted my head to check the lead plane, since I would take over if anything happened to the lead bombardier, there was a terrific jolt as though we had hit a large air pocket. As I learned later it was a 88-mm German anti-aircraft shell hitting our number three engine. The next instant I was flung to the floor of the ship and could not move due to the intensity of the centrifugal force. Don Bragones, the navigator, was behind me but I couldn't look around to see how he was. Before I could think further, everything went blank, and I found myself out in the air, somewhat stunned." From that point Bolen managed to release himself from his flak suit and pull the rip cord. After barely missing the burning target his Group had just bombed he descended to earth. He evaded capture for a week until his luck ran out and he spent the rest of the war in Stallag Luft I.[20]

John Hard, copilot in the 100th Bomb Group, remembers the effort to destroy the oil refineries at Hamburg as his worst experience. At the briefing for the mission, on December 31, the crews expected a "breeze." They were to fly over the North Sea, and hopefully escape the flak. However, when his group crossed the coast headed for Hamburg, "all hell broke loose." He remembers as much ack-ack as he had seen on any mission. One burst knocked out the number two engine and punctured the plane's surface with shrapnel holes. When he entered the bomb run, he also noticed that his ailerons were gone, necessitating his control through use of the rudder and elevator. After dropping the bomb load, his squadron began evasive action. Then he saw one of those sights that remained with him forever: "One B-17 got positioned directly on top of another, neither knowing the other was there. Suddenly the top plane dropped down and impacted on top of the other…The pilots in the top ship were able to maintain some control, so these two piggybacked planes made a slow peel-off and descended in long circles, still tightly impacted into each other, until they were out of sight." He later heard that the top plane kept control and managed a belly landing in Germany, but "at the moment of impact, the top plane broke free, shooting forward over the lower one and crashing well ahead of it. All of the crew in the lower plane were killed, but those in the top were able to get out with minor injuries."

Hard experienced his final excitement as five waves of Focke Wolf-190s and Messerschmitt-109s, flying four abreast, came in at six o'clock and put 100 bullets into his bomber. Fortunately, the damaged B-17 lived up to its reputation and continued to fly, while its gunners destroyed three of the enemy fighters. The bomber limped back across the English Channel just above stalling speed, managing to safely land. He then learned that other crews had reported his plane shot down. While he had survived his worst mission, twelve of the thirty-six planes in his group were not so lucky.[21]

Unfortunately, Hard's observation of the piggyback landing, while a bit unusual, was just one of many air to air disasters observed by anyone who survived 35 missions. Bill Varnedoe, navigator in the 385th Bomb Group, was on his second mission on March, 1, 1945, when he witnessed a horrible midair collision. The formation had just cleared the Belgian coast in route to the railroad marshaling yards at Ulm, in southwest Germany, when a B-17 came up out of a steep dive and struck another fortress near the rear of the radio room, cutting the aircraft in half. He describes the horrifying sight as he observed the two halves: "As I focused on the front half, which was sliding to the left and dropping and was now mighty close to us on our level, I could clearly see the pilot, Chuck Ambruster, looking back over his shoulder trying to see what was happening...Armbruster's front half went into a flat spin and disappeared into the clouds, so near below. It was very eerie seeing all that metal ripping apart only yards away, but without making a sound, as in a silent movie." Then followed "another lasting image...of the radio operator falling out of Ambruster's plane—without his parachute. I believe the whole thing was over in less than fifteen seconds, but that sequence is very vivid in my memory to this day."[22]

The final four months of the European war were similar in terms of mission experiences to the preceding months, with one significant difference. The Luftwaffe was not a serious threat on most missions. Experienced pilots were gone, and even when Luftwaffe commanders wanted to fly, they could not due to the impact of the oil war on air operations. Yet, the sky was still very deadly, and in his memoirs, Bill Varnedoe comments that "The twelve B-17's lost from the 385th during my tour were just as lost as any downed earlier." While German fighter opposition was not what it had been in 1943 and 1944, sporadic fighter opposition was pressed by the Germans with just as much determination." Like other airmen he believed "the weather became more deadly late in the war, since there were so many of us milling around in the soup." Also, missions were more frequent in the last days. Varnedoe put in twenty-six missions in only fifty-six days. He once flew on ten consecutive missions, with eight of that number on consecutive days.[23]

The most serious obstacle the Eighth Air Force faced in those final days was flak. The Germans had removed their ack-ack batteries from less essential targets, and concentrated on protecting key targets such as oil. Also, ack-ack crews had learned from the past and increased their accuracy as the war wound down.

In terms of the overall strategy in the Spring of 1945, the Eighth Air Force complemented the war on the ground with broad destruction of German military capacity and morale. This meant more indiscriminate "blind bombing" that was not that much different from the area bombing practiced by the British. Hitler was stubborn and determined to resist allied pressures on him to end the war, and it appeared that he still had the support of a majority of his people. In a combination of efforts to convince the German government of the futility of continuing the war and to break down civilian morale, the Americans joined the British in giving less attention to strictly military targets.

While neither commanders in upper Air Forces echelons nor in Eighth Air Force headquarters officially endorsed area bombing, possible German civilian casualties were less and less a concern. This was especially true after the Ardennes offensive, and the desire of both allied bomber commands to find the "keystone" or vital center that would convince the Germans of the futility of continuing the war. When Berlin once again became a major target, Spaatz was reported to have stated, "Hit oil if possible. If not, hit Berlin—center of city."[24] Air leaders were disappointed that air power had not truly lived up to its hype, and were desperate to unleash the massive forces in any direction and against any targets that might bring the war to a close. Both the Eighth Air Force and RAF Bomber Command were able to put 1,000 or more bombers in the air on any given mission, and their commanders believed that, if they were ever to demonstrate the worth of air power, the final months of the war was the time.

A good example of the more indiscriminate and more interesting experiments in bombing techniques was the highly classified and extremely dangerous "Aphrodite" program that began in August of 1944 and ended on January 1, 1945. The program was tasked to attack difficult German targets such as heavy concrete sub-pens that had remained impervious to the heaviest bombs. Old, war-weary B-17s and B-24s were stripped of all turrets and armaments and loaded with 20,000 pounds of explosives. They were configured to fly as remotely controlled drones that were guided to the target by radio signals from a mother ship. They generally flew no higher than 2,000 feet.

The two man crews would take off, guide the bomber over England, and just before reaching the coast, bail out as the mother ship took control of the drone to guide it to the target. Unfortunately, the project was largely unsuccessful with only five aircraft coming within five miles of the target. Others were hit by flak or crashed due to mechanical problems. Four pilots were killed, including Joseph Kennedy, brother of the future President. On August 12, he and his radio operator, W.J. Willy, took off at 6:05 p.m. from Dunkeswell, an isolated airfield in Norfolk, in a Navy configured PBY-1, Navy version of the B-24 Liberator, to hit an industrial complex at Mimoyecques, in France. After takeoff, he was to put the aircraft on course, bail out of the bomber, and turn the drone over to the mother ship, a Lockheed Ventura. The formation included two observation aircraft, one flown by General Doolittle. Everything seemed to be going well as Kennedy made a left turn, and had just leveled off, when the aircraft disintegrated. The explosion was so powerful that it flattened a grove of trees at a Suffolk estate below the drone. The largest pieces found were some chunks from the engine blocks. While investigators never located the cause of the explosion, they suspected a problem with the arming wires and/or fuses in the electrical detonation system.[25]

Charles L. Shinault, B-17 pilot in the 96th Bomb Group, volunteered for the project, and on September 17, flew one of the nineteen Aphrodite missions. He recalls that due to the boxes of explosive that filled every inch of space, the two-man crew barely had room in his B-17 to move around. When he went back to the escape hatch prior to bailing out, he had no place to stand, so he had the disconcerting opportunity to sit on boxes of explosives. At the appropriate time he bailed out successfully, but did hurt his head when he hit the edge of the door. The aircraft continued over the channel only to be lost in the haze. Shinault was awarded the Distinguished Flying Cross for participating in the Aphrodite program and went on to complete thirty-five missions.[26]

Air Force officials had hoped to continue the program into 1945, but met resistance from the British, who feared the Germans might retaliate with a similar system, using Luftwaffe aircraft that had been grounded due to a scarcity of fuel and trained pilots. Also, American officials, General Spaatz in particular, hoped to avoid officially indorsing so called "terror bombing" in keeping with stated Air Force policy.[27] The inaccuracy of the remote controlled guided aircraft with its horrendous payload left the real possibility of inerrant hits on nonmilitary targets with a 20,000 pound explosive force second in effect only to the atomic bomb. In years to come the United States was to build on lessons learned in the dark days of 1944, and successfully develop unmanned drones that in many ways helped to revolutionize warfare.

On February 14 and 15, Eighth Air Force joined the RAF in the double barrel bombing of Dresden. Dresden was a major cultural center of Germany and some saw it as a future German capital in the rebuilding of Germany. But it did have synthetic oil, transportation facilities, and several other targets that were on the priority list. What the allies did not know was that the Soviet army, within seventy-five miles of the city, had forced many refugees to find refuge there. On the night of February 13, 800 RAF bombers launched a massive incendiary raid leveling eight square miles of the city, and causing a massive fire storm that took many lives. While unofficial estimates indicated that 135,000 civilians died in the attack, later more accurate figures put the number at 35,000. The following morning, 1,000 Eighth Air Force bombers hit the city again, and in an effort to hit the targets dropped 771 tons of bombs through billows of smoke some 15,000 feet in the air, and in so doing added to the carnage of the previous day. The Eighth Air Force returned to Dresden on the fifteenth with 261 bombers, dropping another 461 tons on synthetic oil plants that had escaped the February 14 bombing.[28]

Raymond Hill was on his last three missions, two to Dresden and one to the oil refinery at Dortmund, Germany. He remembers that, as so often was the case, the smoke and altitude on the bomb run were such as to make it impossible to observe the devastation on the ground. However reality took hold two days after the missions when he read in the *Stars and Stripes* that the city was a "heap of ruins." A correspondent reported that "tens of thousands, many of them refugees who had a small chance to find shelter, had perished in three raids."[29] While he did not know it at that time, Hill had participated in one of the most controversial raids of the war. It became a political issue when reports out of a SHAEF conference indicated that in the future the Allied bombers would "conduct a deliberate campaign of terror." Spaatz quickly informed Arnold that the SHAEF spokesman did not represent USTAF policies.[30]

Of course, even though specific target selection was made by the Combined American and British Strategic Targets Committee (C.S.T.C.), General Eisenhower often superseded decisions where close air to ground support was needed. For example, from February 22 through the end of the month, all available aircraft, at the request of General Eisenhower, launched operation Clarion, directed at German communications which could affect both the economic life of German citizens and the tactical situation of the closing offensive. Included in the operation was destruction of many small towns, which in turn could affect morale. During that period daily missions of more than 1,000 bombers from the Eighth, Ninth, and Fifteenth Air Forces knocked out much of the transportation network in Eastern Germany. As to the effect on morale, the actual impact has never fully been measured. In another SHAEF press conference, a comment was made that the allies were "perhaps...trying to injure the morale of a people who had no morale."[31] The accuracy of that statement remains open to debate.

Due to a combination of bad weather and the concentration of as many available bombers and fighters as possible to turn back the German offensive in the Ardennes, along with continuous use of many aircraft for tactical support of ground troops, many strategic targets were put on hold, consequently giving Germany a breather, and time to replace some industrial losses and increase production of jet aircraft. In fact, although the Luftwaffe had lost many of its most experienced pilots, more than 800 jet aircraft, ME-262s and AR-234s came off the German assembly line, requiring the C.S.T.C. to place jet factories near the top of the priority list.[32] Of course destruction of oil facilities seriously affected the usefulness of the new aircraft. Tank, truck, armored vehicle, and ordinance production, had also increased over the winter months, and dictated that many missions be directed at targets in and around Berlin, Ulm, Kassel, Magdeburg, Vienna, and Nuremburg.

Crews arriving in the final three months of the war found most if not all of these targets on their mission schedules. And, with such targets, came increased accuracy in flak. This was especially true of Berlin. In the years following World War II, when Eighth Air Force veterans assemble and discuss their most memorable missions, the experiences over Berlin whether in 1944 or 1945 always comes into the conversations. Near the top of their list was the mission on March 18, 1945 when a record 1,251 bombers escorted by 645 P-51s attacked two rail centers, two tank and armament plants, and a large industrial complex near Berlin.

Varnedoe knew he was in for a rough day when the briefing officer pulled the curtain back. "We all 'ohed' and 'ahed'" he said, "for the black tape on the map led to Big B, Berlin." His group was to hit the railroad in the heart of the city. True to form, the flak was intense. He said, "I saw a cluster of six flak bursts at our level. Shortly, there were six more, closer. The next six were very close. And I could see the following six would intercept our flight path. But we were on the bomb run and could not take any [evasive] action." Just as he expected, the next cluster hit his plane and damaged one engine. Fortunately the damage was not critical and the crippled bomber continued to the target. Then, as the pilot attempted to turn the aircraft sharply after the bomb run, the turn was so tight the aircraft was "literally slung out of formation…right back through the flak zone again." Their luck did hold and the bomber did make it safely back to its home base at Greater Ashfield. But, in looking back today, Varnedoe remembers that experience and the deadly flak indiscriminately hitting bombers as evidence that "fate does not always hit the OTHER CREW, I realized that my number could come up at any time," he said.[33]

Holcombe, flying as flight engineer in the 305th Bomb Group, has much the same feeling as he looks back today at that mission, especially as it related to flak. He remembers how beautiful the Sunday was as he approached the target. It was the kind of day he would like to have enjoyed "back home in Anniston, Alabama, not over Berlin. All of the ack-ack gunners could see us clear as a bell," he remembers. "As we approached the target, flak knocked out our number one engine by cutting the oil lines. We could not get it feathered due to loss of oil, resulting in a wind milling prop. We immediately dropped our bombs and, at the same time, took a flak hit in the number two engine which let gasoline pour out." In a familiar scenario, the crippled B-17 fell out of formation and struggled to hold altitude while the crew hoped enemy planes would not discover their plight. Fortunately, it was 1945, and not a year earlier when the Luftwaffe was at its best and frequently picked off the stragglers. Holcombe continues, "we were going down pretty fast...I started to jettison everything that would lighten the plane to help maintain altitude with two engines. We dumped fifty- caliber machine guns, ammunition, and anything that looked heavy. We even salvoed (sic) the ball turret." He credits the skill of the navigator for steering the plane back across Germany, "hiding in every cloud bank, and missing military installations."

After guiding the bomber across the American lines the pilot spotted an abandoned fighter strip in Belgium and made a "fairly decent landing." When Holcombe left the aircraft he immediately kissed the ground. After a day of rest, he went back to look at the war weary bomber and counted ninety-seven holes that were two inches or larger, one as large as his head. He also experienced another familiar event as he returned to his base with the help of Belgian citizens and the Red Cross. He discovered that he was listed as "Missing in Action," and that his belongings had already been sent to a warehouse.[34]

Bill Thompson, copilot in the 100th Bomb Group, also remembers that mission to Berlin for some very special reasons. Unlike Holcombe, who survived his encounter with the Luftwaffe, Thompson fell victim to the best the Germans had to offer, as new technology entered the air war in the form of jet fighters. His crew was on its sixth mission and its first as a lead crew. They were flying in the low squadron, and since the Group Command Pilot was flying in Thompson's copilot place, he flew as rear gunner. As his group approached Berlin, it was attacked by six to ten Me-262s. According to the Group intelligence report, "the jets came from five to seven o'clock low to level using contrails and cloud banks for cover...Three E/A (enemy aircraft) seemed to go for the lead A/C (aircraft)...One broke away to the left when seventy-five yards back, another broke to the right at about the same time and the third came into the formation and broke away toward ten o'clock and down. The lead bomber [Thompson's plane] and its left wing were both set afire by this attack. A few minutes later, this same attack was repeated by three Me-262s, from 0630 level. At almost the same instant, the #2 plane in the high squadron broke in two between the door and the waist window, while the #3 plane in the low element was hit and couldn't stay in position. The last plane in the formation, "tail end Charlie," blew up.

In the midst of the melee Thompson's pilot, Lt. Paul De Weerdt, made a 180-degree turn and dropped from 30,000 to 20,000 feet. He had flown about fifty miles when the bomber took a second hit, and a few minutes later exploded. In recounting the excitement of that brief time before bail out, Thompson remembers, "I was a little slow in getting out because I went back to my tail position twice before jumping. Once to get some fruit drops [and] an orange and the last time to get my chest pack. I delayed opening for at least 25,000 ft. because we had been told of guys being shot at in chutes." Thompson and eight crewmen safely descended to the ground. However, their efforts to avoid the enemy were brief and they were soon captured. After some interrogation, they joined the ranks of the POWs in Stalag Luft I, where they remained for the remainder of the war.[35]

Owen O'Rourke alternated between the B-24 waist and tail gunner positions in the 457th Bomb Group, and on the Berlin mission learned to respect both German ack-ack crews and German jets. He saw the jets for the first time and was amazed at their speed. He echoed the view of others that the flak over Berlin was as bad as any in the war. He remembers the whole experience as his most grueling day with 12 hours in the air, his longest mission.[36]

The Eighth Air Force visited Berlin for the last time on March 28, when 900 heavy bombers escorted by eight groups of F-51s attacked the tank factory and armament plant near the center of the city, in addition to other targets of opportunity. In spite of the fact that bombs were obviously causing a great deal of collateral damage due to the proximity of the target to the heart of the city, airmen who went there had no feelings of guilt about their mission. They had seen too many of their friends go down over such targets, and had witnessed the horrors in the air in the spring of 1945 that helped them realize that the war had gone on far too long, and any effort to bring it to a conclusion was fair game.

The Luftwaffe made one last effort against heavy bombers on April 7, sending up 250 fighters, including fifty jets, against 1,200

Fortresses and Liberators attacking two explosive plants, oil storage depots, and an ordinance depot in central and northern Germany. Dedicated to the end, that last remnant of a once proud German air force shot down fifteen bombers, but at a cost of sixty fighters including a few jets. For Varnedoe, the mission was far from ordinary. In bombing the ordinance warehouse at Gustow, his group attracted the attention of three ME-109s. He watched in horror as an Me-109 that had been hit by B-17 tail gunners in his bomber and another next to him crashed into another plane. Following that incident Varnedoe's B-17 lost its oxygen system and was forced to drop to a lower level. The pilot managed to bring the bomber back to England, having experienced the last major air battle of the European war. Varnedoe later stated that he "would have been irritated if anyone had said the air war was no longer hazardous." Many German aircraft were seen in the remaining weeks, but most were on the ground and easy targets for American fighters.[37]

On April 25, 1945, 250 Eighth Air Force B-17s and an equal number of B-24s escorted by P-51s flew the last bombing mission of the European war. They bombed the Skoda armament works and an airfield in Pilzen, Czechslovakia, and other targets near Salzburg. George Owen, flight engineer in the 406th Bomb Group, was on his tenth mission to Salzburg. His mission was called off while in route to Austria, but on the return trip to his base at Attlebridge, he saw a B-17 get hit by flak. It went down and all but two of the crew were lost. It was the last bomber shot down, and later became the subject of a book by Thomas Childers, *Wings in the Morning*.[38]

Charles Patterson, 305th BG, arrived at Chevelston on April 3, 1945, in time to fly four missions before the war ended. His first three were uneventful, but he would never forget his fourth and last when he flew on that Eighth Air Force's final bombing mission. He was flying in the navigator's seat, since regular navigators were not needed at that stage of the war. He merely had to release the bombs when the lead bombardier released his, a seemingly easy task. He released the bombs as instructed and the aircraft veered away from the target. The last bombs had been dropped on Germany, in World War II—except one! When the radio operator checked the bomb bay, he discovered that one bomb had not dropped and was hanging by one end of two shackle devices. Patterson had no choice but to crawl into the bomb bay to attempt to release the bomb. Just as he reached the bomb bay, to his relief, the bomb dropped. However his excitement did not end. As he made his way back to his position, the pilot called out that he was feathering two engines due to a fire, and the crew should prepare to bail out. Patterson headed for the front escape hatch, but just as he was ready to release the hatch, he heard the second good news of the day. The fire was out and the pilot hoped to make it out of enemy territory. The bomber, as so many others had done over the past two years, limped back to England on two engines. Patterson then saw something that has haunted him to this day. The seat he had vacated to prepare to bail out had a flak hole in it that was about four inches in diameter.[39]

In November 1942, General Asa Duncan, an Alabamian, was the first commander of the Eighth Air Force, and the first to die in the line of duty. On April 25, 1945, three years later, a young sergeant, 18-year-old Charles Patterson, another Alabamian, who was completing high school at the time of Duncan's ill-fated flight, in all likelihood, dropped the last bomb on a German target—and he very nearly had the distinction of becoming the last fatality as the Third Reich that Hitler had said "would last a thousand years" crumbled before the allied forces.

7

Evasion, Capture and the Stalag

As we looked toward town, we saw the German flag flying above City Hall. We saw the German flag being lowered and the Stars and Stripes go up in its place...This was such an emotional moment that it made goose bumps cover my body.

Roy Davidson, 94th Bomb Group

On September 18, 1944, four days after giving birth to a baby girl, Frances Bolen received a telegram from the Adjutant General of the Army Air Forces. In capital letters it read:

REPORT JUST RECEIVED THROUGH THE INTERNATIONAL RED CROSS STATES THAT YOUR HUSBAND SECOND LIEUTENANT FRANK S. BOLEN IS A PRISONER OF WAR OF THE GERMAN GOVERNMENT. LETTER OF INFORMATION FOLLOWS FROM PROVOST MARSHAL GENERAL

The day was also the second anniversary of Frances' marriage to Lt. Frank Bolen. Like many other anxious wives, she did find some good news in the terse announcement, in that he was "captured" and not dead. She later reminisced that she believed he would return. "I never doubted," she said. "I have said many times that I either had great faith or I didn't have enough sense to really figure it out-but I knew Frank would come back." On October 28, Frances received a letter from the Army Air Force War Division, which justified her faith. It reiterated, that her husband was indeed interned as a prisoner of war, and on December 7, a letter from Frank dated September 18, three months earlier, indicated that he was "okay." Finally, on February 24, 1945, five months after he was interned in Stalag Luft I as a *Kregie (*short for *Kregefrangenon,* the German name for prisoners of war), Bolen received his first letter from his wife and the news that he had a baby daughter.[1]

Thousands of other families joined Frances in the anxious months of not knowing the fate of their loved ones, and though the circumstances and sequence of events would vary, the anxieties and uncertainties were every bit as real, made worse by the dearth of mail or other information that might have eased their concerns. And unfortunately many anxious families, unlike Frances Bolen, received a different type of telegram, that instead of joy, brought sadness and the dreaded news of the permanent loss of a loved one.

Eighth Air Force airmen who experienced captivity in Europe shared a camaraderie beset with dangers and death- defying situations. For most, the road to the Stalag began with a similar sequence of events. That was until capture. Then, each captive faced his personal and often harrowing ordeals, with the will to survive foremost in his thoughts and actions.

Each story began at a base in England where the anxious airman prepared for "one more mission" that would take him one step closer to completion of the mandatory number of twenty-five missions required for rotation home (changed to thirty-five in late 1944). The day began with the usual early wake-up, followed by the normal preliminaries, breakfast, briefing, preparation for takeoff, and then:

Enormous relief as his bomber cleared the runway and broke through the overcast, and realizing that once again he had escaped death, that could have come in an explosion and ball of fire or a midair collision, a fate suffered by so many crews.

Feeling of security as the bomber located its own group surrounded by hundreds of other heavily armed bombers and fighters creating what appeared to be an invincible shield of protection.

Tension and renewed fear as the formation crossed the coast of France and flew deeper and deeper into hostile air space over Hitler's Fortress Europe. Prior to January 1944, a fear greatly enhanced when fighter escorts were forced to return to England due to their lack of fuel range.

Feelings of both excitement and apprehension when Luftwaffe fighters suddenly appeared and began to scout the formation like a wolf pack selecting its prey.

For many airmen, such security was not to be. The pilot, realizing that the crippled aircraft was going down, either attempted a crash landing, or ordered the crew to bail out. For those that bailed out, the trip down by parachute was an experience of indescribable quietness mixed with a terrible fear of what was ahead. The impact with the ground brought a sudden jolt and the realization that for the moment at least they were still alive.

Pilots electing to ride their planes down had their own share of excitement, with each incident entirely different from any other. In both situations the men who set foot safely on the ground found themselves in hostile territory with one thought foremost in mind-how to evade capture. While some were successful, others were apprehended either immediately after stepping on enemy soil, or after a period of evasion, were caught and imprisoned in one of the German Stalags.

Eighth Air Force officers who had the misfortune to be among the 21,000 of their number to be captured became part of 45,000 POWs interned in Europe. Many spent the remainder of the war in either Stalag Luft I, near Barth in northern Germany bordering the Baltic Sea, or Stalag Luft III, west of Berlin, near Frankfurt. These camps were controlled primarily by the Luftwaffe for internment of American and Allied officers. As POW camps in Germany went, they had better overall conditions than other Stalags. Enlisted airmen were usually sent to Stalag Luft IV at Grosstychow in East Prussia, or Stalag Luft VI at Bankau, also in East Prussia. Some officers and airmen were also sent to Stalag Lufg XVIII B at Krems, Austria. While prison experiences for the enlisted men were similar to those of officers, they received less attention from the Luftwaffe, and their overall conditions were usually worse.

Prison camp conditions were supposed to follow the guidelines of the *Geneva Convention Relating to the Treatment of Prisoners of War,* signed in 1929 by the nations of the world. In fact, the convention directed that the agreements be posted in a prominent place in each camp. Generally, the Germans made an attempt to follow the basic guidelines of the document, but often with loose interpretation to suit their own convenience. Lawson Corley knew that the conditions at Stalag Luft III violated most of the Geneva guidelines, and while there, made some notes on the back of some Gin Rummy cards that were later used as part of the evidence at the Nuremberg trials. Quoting specific provisions of the guidelines, he wrote: "the conditions were untenable and a protest of the strongest nature is hereby registered for present and future consideration." His diet, he wrote, "was less than that required for basic metabolism and will inevitably lead to loss of much weight and starvation under the present unhygienic and unhealthy circumstances." He became a living example of his statement following release, when he stepped on the scale, and realized he had lost fifty pounds during his time in the Stalag.[2] Under the best of conditions, POW life was an agonizing ordeal tolerated one day at a time, and captives lived for the day they would be released.

After surviving the terrible ordeal of an exploding Bomber over Metz, France, on September 9, 1944, Frank Bolen managed to guide his parachute safely over the burning inferno created a few minutes earlier by the bombs from his formation. As he struck the ground, he sprained his right ankle severely, but was able to hobble to the brush on the edge of an island. Knowing that the Germans were surely looking for him, he began efforts at escape and evasion that he had learned in survival training in England.

Bolen knew that he was on the Rhine river and also knew that the nearest Allied forces were at least 150 miles to the west, and that the border between France and the Germany was perhaps 75 to 100 miles to the southwest. He did not want to fall into the hands of German civilians or the German Gestapo, either of which might have killed him, or at best made his life miserable. He had heard horror stories of unlucky airmen who fell into the hands of angry German civilians and were beaten, hung or pitchforked by their captives. Although no official records or accurate numbers of victims of such tragedies exist, they were in the thousands. German officials incited the population against the airmen by placing propaganda in newspapers and over the air waves referring to the Americans as terror fliers (*Terrorflieger*) or as air gangsters (*Luftgangster*). Propaganda Minister Joseph Goebbels and SS Commander Heinrich Himmler did nothing to discourage the actions of disgruntled civilians seeking revenge.[3]

After locating a rowboat anchored on the island, Bolen rowed to the shore. The next morning he began a ten-mile trip to the north toward the city of Worms, but first he had to cross a loosely guarded bridge that would put him on the west side of the river. When he arrived at the bridge, he started across the river, but had gone but a short distance when he encountered a problem. "Half way over," he said, "I met a German guard patrolling his post who stopped and looked straight into my face. I prayed reverently with the blood pounding through my veins. I continued on without flinching. Apparently satisfied, and to my relief, the guard clomped off in the other direction." Bolen then continued through the town, and over the next three days, with no food other than a chocolate ration and what food he could find in the fields he limped on for about 30 miles, growing weaker and suffering from a sprained ankle that had doubled its normal size.

On the morning of the sixth day Bolen entered the outskirts of a small German village, named Lambsheim. "I had been without water for three days," he said, "and decided that, even at the expense of probable capture, I would enter this town ...and quench my thirst ... Summoning all the courage I could muster, I walked down the street toward the railroad station. Passing a group of older men, I nodded to them and was not too surprised when they acknowledged me. I had gone about five city blocks before finding a water hydrant where I drank all I wanted, then filled my cellophane bottle."

On his seventh day of evasion near the town of Speyerdorf, his luck ran out. Two German soldiers with a girl companion that he tried to ignore were not fooled, and one of the soldiers yelled "Halt" in French. Bolen was quickly persuaded as to his next course of action by a long-nosed Lugar one of the soldiers pointed in his direction. Fortunately for Bolen the soldiers were members of the German Luftwaffe, and after treating him with a degree of decency, turned him over to authorities. His captivity in Stalag Luft I soon followed. There he would reside until the end of the war.[4]

Lawson Corley's evasion was short lived, and he remembers events as one painful experience after another. After bailing out of his burning B-24 and descending in a damaged oscillating parachute, he landed on his back, cracked two vertebrae, ruptured his right kidney, and damaged a spleen. He did not expect things to get much worse, but he was mistaken. Before he could find refuge in the Belgian underground, the German field police with the help of bloodhounds found him along with his flight engineer Walter Niespodziewany, who had been attending his wounds. They were taken to what Corley referred to as a Gestapo "dungeon" where they were beaten and interrogated. Corley knew that he must resist interrogation efforts due to his knowledge of the upcoming invasion. He succeeded, but in the process suffered the loss of eleven teeth, a broken cheek, a left eye knocked out of its socket, and a busted left ear drum. When the interrogators gave up on efforts to obtain information they took all of his possessions and transported him to a hospital in Brussels, the first stop he would make en route to Stalag Luft III.[5]

Kenneth McCaleb and Roy Davidson were two of the 600 air crewmen to go down in the second raid on the ball-bearing factory at Schweinfurt. McCaleb parachuted out of his B-17, made a very hard landing and was knocked unconscious for about thirty minutes. He awoke to find himself surrounded by peasants with pitchforks. Fortunately, they turned him over to the Luftwaffe, and a week later he was interned in Stalag Luft III.[6]

While Davidson eventually joined McCaleb in Stalag Luft III, he took a round-about route to get there, and in so doing completed one of the classic evasion efforts in Eighth Air Force history.

After his successful crash landing in a French pasture, Davidson broke his crew up into small groups, and leaving a severely wounded member in an open field where he would hopefully be rescued, he and three other crew members, navigator Al Faudie, turret gunner Fred Krueger, and a wounded crew member, Richard Mungenasst, began their efforts to distance themselves from the burning aircraft. Not sure as to whether they had crashed in Germany or France, they hid in some bushes until after dark and then began to walk in a westerly direction. The walk and especially the near encounter with a raging bull, prompted Davidson to leave the wounded Mungenasst beside a farmhouse where he could get help the following morning.

Davidson and his remaining crew members began a hike through woods and over beds of wire fences, not knowing where they were. When they came upon a farmhouse, their cold and tired condition prompted them to seek some rest in a barn. Their rest came to an abrupt end when a young girl gathering eggs from the barn discovered the two airmen and let out a "blood curdling scream." After a difficult encounter with the girl's father, who appeared with a shotgun in his hand, and after attempts at exchanging broken French with him, they finally persuaded him that they were Americans. Now Davidson knew they were in France, and a few moments later they were treated to a breakfast of scrambled eggs.

Following a brief stay in the French home, Davidson, along with Faudie and Krueger, were introduced to the French underground. Three men arrived in a truck, gave them civilian clothes, and then transported them to the little town of Epernay. After evading a German road block and successfully arriving in the town the airmen arrived at a home of the area chief of the French underground until arrangements for escape could be made. There, Faudie was separated from Davidson and Krueger. After a couple days of French hospitality and relative comfort, the two airmen were taken to a local restaurant to meet with French underground members who would aide them in their efforts to return to England. They were then equipped with a new identity card with a new picture and new name, along with clothes that helped them blend in with the population. Their escape route was to be by way of a train trip to Paris, then to Spain, and finally to England.

On his trip to Paris, Davidson "expected arrest at any minute." It was on a train loaded with hostile German soldiers and civilians, and he was advised by the French underground that since he could not speak German, he should just hand his I.D. card to the German inspector who patrolled the train. "One problem" he said, "was to keep people from talking to us; so Fernandez {French escort} gave us a magazine so we could pretend to be reading...We handed our train ticket and I.D. card to the German at the gate and were admitted to the train...An aisle ran down one side of the train. It was frightening at first to rub shoulders with German soldiers. I felt that one would arrest me at any minute, but I finally realized that I looked just like any other French man...Unfortunately for me, a talkative woman sat beside me. I was pretending to read my magazine when the woman began talking to me in French. I had no idea what she was talking about. I assumed she wanted to see my magazine, so I gave it to her and immediately pretended to go to sleep all the way to Paris."

After several hours of rail travel he arrived in Paris. There, as instructed and in true spy novel fashion, he met a woman who he embraced, and then followed. "This was a weird feeling," he remembers, and "I had to pinch myself as we started following this strange woman in the subway. It seemed so much like something in the movies, yet it was happening to me." The mysterious woman then turned the airmen over to a high-ranking member of the underground. He directed that they act drunk as he checked them into a hotel. There they awaited instructions for a train to Spain. The next day, Davidson was taken to an apartment house where he joined Krueger again and three British airmen also awaiting transport to Spain. Then came bad news. Transportation to Spain could only be arranged for three men. At that time the United States Government was paying $500.00 to the underground for return of airmen, while the British government paid $600.00. Therefore, since Britain was the highest bidder, the three British airmen were on their way to Spain, while Davidson and Krueger would have to take the frightening trip back to Epernay, and await a different route back to England.

Up to that point Davidson and Krueger had followed the textbook type of evasion they had heard about before they left England, and they had no reason not to believe that eventually they would soon be back at Bury St. Edmunds with the 94th Bomb Group. However, they returned to the hospitality of their French friends in Epernay at a time when the Gestapo was closing in on the underground. A few days after their arrival, their hosts received news that indeed the Gestapo had arrested members of the underground, and it was only a matter of time until the airmen would be discovered. Quickly, they were removed to a different house, where they stayed until arrangements were made to transport them to England. They were put on yet another train, this time to the seaport village of Quimper, where they were to catch a fishing boat that would rendezvous with a submarine. After two difficult nights on a train, they found that the mission had been cancelled. Once again, Davidson and Krueger made the trip back to Paris, where they waited until new arrangements could be made. After a few days they were back in Quimper where they received the news they were expecting; a scheduled rendezvous with a submarine and the long awaited return to British soil. But first they had to make the treacherous journey by boat to the rendezvous point with the submarine.

After a trip by truck to the shore, the two Americans and about thirty-five other men boarded a fishing boat for the trip into the channel. About three hours from the rendezvous time the engines suddenly stopped. Davidson's heart sank when an inspection by the boat captain revealed a flooded engine room. That meant that the boat was not only dead in the water but was also sinking. Davidson remembers the next few harrowing moments as the most frightening he experienced. "The weather was well below freezing for this was late January, and the cold Atlantic wind and weather seemed to go right through you...The captain put up sails and the prevailing winds were blowing us toward land... The Frenchmen all gave up and prepared to meet their maker." But Davidson, Krueger and a British pilot were not quite ready to quit. "We were praying too," he said, "but at the same time Krueger and I found a two-gallon bucket and started bailing water. While we bailed, the captain put up sails and the boat slowly headed toward shore."

Davidson remembers that "several times we were most fortunate and just barely missed some protruding rocks. Had we hit them the boat would have crashed with no hope for us. At 8:00 a.m. we sighted land at a point called 'Devil's Mouth,' where many shipwrecks had occurred, The ship was six inches above water and every wave rolled across the deck...We soon reached shore, which was a steep cliff. We climbed to the top and started walking, but we were picked up by a German patrol which was sent out to look for us. By now we really didn't care, for we were so thankful to be alive." For Roy Davidson and others on that boat, "the war was over." But as Davidson and Krueger embarked on their trip to prison, they faced new obstacles as they attempted to convince their captors that they were American airmen and not spies. This was understandable since they were in civilian clothes and had fake identification cards identifying them as French citizens.

The two airmen were taken by train to Rennes for interrogation and the beginning of confinement. Davidson spent the next two weeks trying to convince the Gestapo that he was not a spy. Alternating questioning, the Gestapo officers and the "beautiful woman" they had been warned about in escape and evasion classes did all they could to obtain information that went beyond the Geneva Convention restrictions of "name, rank, and serial number." Much that Davidson told them was fabricated. He and Krueger were very careful not to reveal the names of the French underground that had helped them to escape and one of Davidson's most satisfying memories was that no Frenchmen suffered as a result of his interrogation.

After two weeks in three prisons at Rennes, Davidson and Krueger, were moved to Gestapo headquarters in Paris. There, they were deloused, fingerprints were taken, and they were confined in the Fresnes prison, where they were placed in a very small cell with four Frenchmen Over the next two months he went through several interrogations as the Gestapo was still not convinced that he was who he said he was. On one occasion, he chiseled his name, branch of service, serial number, and the month, in the prison wall just in case he disappeared. As he saw Frenchmen being escorted out of the prison for either further imprisonment or worse, execution, he feared that his family would never know his fate.

Three months after his capture, Davidson was separated from Krueger and sent to Weisbaden, Germany, where he was placed in the city jail with an American navigator. Finally, in April 1944, a Gestapo officer interrogated Davidson again, this time to find out once and for all whether or not he was a spy. In the interrogation he asked the Gestapo officer what he wanted to know. He was told that he would give him a simple test to determine whether or not he was who he said he was. As Davidson remembers "He said he would give each of us a sheet of paper and each of us was to answer three questions. When finished he would turn the papers face up and, if they matched, it would prove I was a soldier and would be sent to a POW camp. If they did not match, that would prove I was a spy." The questions were about Davidson's former base. When the papers were turned face up Davidson had correctly answered two of the questions, but missed the third that asked the name of his commanding officer. While Davidson had answered that Colonel Castle was his commander, the interrogator informed him the correct answer was General Davis. Then he was asked when he was shot down, and Davidson replied October 14, 1943. The officer said, "that explained his answer since he had no way of knowing that Colonel Castle was shot down and killed on a December raid on Berlin." Much to his relief, Davidson had convinced the Gestapo officer that he truly was a soldier and not a spy. Two days later, Davidson was on his way to be processed as a legitimate POW He remembered that as bad as POW status was, he was delighted to be recognized as such and to hear the "Germans say in their heavy accented English, *"For you, zee var iss ofer."*[7]

When Corley arrived at Stalag Luft III on May 25, 1944, he was not the only POW from his hometown—Birmingham Alabama—to share the reality of prison life in that famous German prison. Davidson, who had arrived a month earlier, had been a schoolmate of his at Woodlawn High School in Birmingham. Although the two men had been a year apart in school, they recognized each other, and felt some comfort in knowing that they shared a common background—one to which they very much hoped to return. Corley then went through the usual interrogation by other Krieges in his compound to assure them that he was not a German in disguise who may have been planted in the camp. He easily passed the test when Davidson recognized his former classmate and identified him to the other POWs.[8]

Lieutenants Bolen and Thompson were incarcerated in Stalag Luft I, the second of the two camps reserved for British and American officers. Bolen was confined there after seven days of evasion. While the location of Luft I was different, the dismal and very depressing conditions were very similar. A fellow POW, Donald Brzones, reflected on the dark days there and remembered that, "We had little to do, little to eat, much to think about."[9]

On March 18, 1945, Bill Thompson, B-17 pilot in the in the 100th Bomb Group, was forced to bail out over Falkenberry on the outskirts of Berlin, and landed in a pine tree, unhooked his chute, and fell 20 feet to the ground. He walked two nights until he found a rail depot. Following a night hiding in a hay stack, he hopped on a passenger car of a train pulling out of the railway station. He changed to a freight train in Stettin and rode it for a night and day until disembarking at Hamburg. While walking in the direction where he believed Patton's Army to be, he was caught by a couple of Volkstrums. He was then taken through a village of jeering farmers before being locked up in a fenced enclosure with what appeared to be prison laborers.

He was eventually turned over to the Luftwaffe, and following an agonizing trip by train, during which time he feared strafing by American aircraft as much as did his captors, he arrived at a Luftwaffe base. There, a "polite briefing officer" interrogated him, attempting to obtain information about the 100th Bomb Group. Thompson described the officer as, "very courteous and spoke perfect English. He had been a U.S. tour guide. After he was sure that I would not answer all of his questions, he smiled, reached for a looseleaf notebook and read me all there was to know about the 100th. Lots more than I knew." From the Luftwaffe interrogation center, Thompson went by train to Barth and his prison home for the next three months.[10]

Memories in one's life often fade with time, or more often take on a different form. However, some events are so imbedded in the subconscious that even time will not erase them. Such was the case with many prisoners of war who were imprisoned in the German Stalags. Accounts of the POWs, even after a half century or more, are amazingly similar in details and impressions. Even such minutiae as the positioning of furnishings in prison barracks are almost exact from POW to POW. Bill Thompson's memory of room arrangement in Luft I and the cooking and eating utensils was almost identical to that of Frank Bolen. Memories of that camp were also similar to those shared by Roy Davidson, Kenneth McCaleb, and Lawson Corley in Luft III.

Regardless of the camp or time of confinement, the *Kregies,* survived through their own ingenuity and perseverance. Davidson quotes a former POW, Thomas P.Griffen, and his description of what it was like to be a prisoner of war: "To be a prisoner of war is to suffer the agony of rehabilitation. Suddenly you are in an alien world. It is the frustration of trying to cope. Trying to fit into a society that suddenly seems foreign. A society unable to relate to your experiences. It is the resentment you immediately feel for those who have never felt what you have. They will never see what you have seen. Their personal problems pale by comparison. It is the recurring nightmares that plague you for the rest of your life. It is the nagging question, "what was it all for? What good did it do? Who cares?" Griffen went on to answer his own question and believed there was a purpose. "I believe the ex-prisoner of war has a much clearer perspective of what is real and who is genuine," he said. "Perhaps he better understands what really is important in life—I do"[11] Other former POWs strongly echo Griffen's analysis.

When the airmen arrived at their Stalag, they were given a hot shower and clean clothes, furnished by the International Red Cross. Throughout their captivity the POWs were grateful for Red Cross packages, without which their life would have been more miserable than it was. They also received toilet articles, a fork and spoon, a tin cup, and a Red Cross food parcel. They were then assigned to a barracks and room, and while room sizes and total number of occupants would vary, at best they were tight quarters. The men generally slept on triple bunk beds with seven wooden slats (in the great escape of April 1944, the bed slats were used to support the walls in the escape tunnel) to support the mattresses. They normally received two blankets and a wool overcoat. On the very cold winter nights, the overcoat served as an additional blanket.

In each room, an iron stove provided a minuscule amount of heat and was positioned in such a way as to provide some semblance of heat to two rooms. The room had a single table, benches, and a cabinet. Windows had outside shutters that were closed every night. The doors to the barracks were also closed every night, usually around 9:00, and secured with a wooden board. A single light hung from a drop cord in the center of the room. *Kregies* made their own plates and some cooking utensils with table knives and #1 tin cans that had contained powdered milk or klim (milk spelled backwards). The latrine was located two or three buildings from the barracks. It contained a shower that seldom had hot water, where Octagon soap and scrub brushes were available.[12]

To coordinate day-to-day activities and to collaborate where possible against the German captors, each barracks was organized. Bolen describes the organization in Stalag Luft I: "There was a barracks commander and vice commander. Each room had a room commander who was selected by the occupants of that room. At all times during the day we pulled duty which we called Goon Guard." That is, we had a roster of all the men in the barracks and for a period of one day an American was stationed at each end of the barracks inside the door. His duty was to watch for approaching Germans and then alert the barracks in a loud voice saying, "Goon up. This was the signal to hide any contraband articles or information that might be out."[13]

"Daily we had many Germans visiting and checking our progress," said Thompson. He said that the POWs found many ways to have fun. We would "get up at night and scrape boards on the outside wall out the window behind our 55 gallon toilets. This always aroused the camp lights on, dogs barking and guards running. Of course all of us would act asleep by then. Other fun was had by not covering down at check times; this prevented the guards from counting us."[14]

Each morning and afternoon, the men would line up to be counted. If someone was missing, the *Kregies* would stay in formation until the missing person was accounted for. At times, the POWs were quite hungry by the time the roll call was finished. Regardless of the time for their meal, their food provided basic subsistence, and that was about all. The "Geneva Convention" stipulated that POWs were to be fed food equivalent to what the captors of like rank received. The Germans never came close to meeting that standard, and had it not been for the Red Cross parcels delivered once a week survival would have been difficult. During the Battle of the Bulge in late 1944, supply lines for German food were cut and the Red Cross parcels were cut in half. On occasions, the Red Cross would inspect the camp. How the camps passed the inspection was a mystery.

While their daily food ration may have varied depending on availability, the POWs usually received an allowance of two cups of "fake" coffee per day to drink with two slices of black bread, a couple of boiled potatoes, and once a week, helpings of vegetables such as cabbage, carrots, kohlrabi. For protein, they received small helpings of horse meat, cheese, or blood sausage. They supplemented this meager diet with the Red Cross package consisting of spam, corned beef, salmon, one pound of sugar, klim, a box of prunes or raisins, margarine, chocolate D-bar, and cigarettes. The only time they received enough to eat was at Christmas when the Red Cross parcel contained traditional Christmas items such as roast turkey, cranberry sauce and plum pudding.[15]

The *Kregies* were quite innovative and could make many recipes out of their meager food allotment. Davidson described the Christmas of 1944 when two *Kregies* used their prunes to make homemade liquor. "This made them so drunk that they walked past the 'No Man's Land,' climbed two ten-foot high barbed wire fences and escaped temporarily. When they tried to climb the fence again to return to their compound, they were caught. As a result of that incident the Kregies lost their ration of fruit for a period of time. When the camp commanding officer pleaded with the Germans, the restriction on fruit was lifted, and the Kriegies made no more booze.[16]

Kregies were so desperate, especially in early 1945 that they ate anything, such as beans with worms in them. On one occasion, the

POWs in Luft III received a large portion of cheese with mold on it. One hungry POW ate the mold and became deathly sick. The POWs all agreed that the number one topic constantly on their mind was food, with girls a distant second. McCaleb remembers that the men in his compound formed a "club of sorts; We promised that when the war was ended and we returned to the United States, each of us would send $50.00 worth of food to each of the others. The fellow from the ranch in Texas would send everyone a side of beef; the fellow from Wisconsin would send cheese; the one from Hershey, Pennsylvania, would send chocolate, and I was to send strawberry and blackberry jam. None of us kept his promise." He went on to say that on the troop ship home "five of us [each] bought a 24-bar carton of chocolate candy. Six of us ate the 120 candy bars in 24 hours."[17]

Depression was one of the POW's biggest enemies. To combat it they sought any possible diversion, especially to erase the nagging thought that the war would never end. They hungered for outside news and, fortunately, in both camps, some enterprising POW managed to hide a radio that kept them in touch with the BBC. "Each day we had underground radio reports of Allied fronts," said Thompson, "and we kept this info published on our large map in the barracks foyer."[18] Through what they heard on the radio and the sight of huge bomber formations passing over their camp, the POWs had no doubts as to the direction the war was taking.

Even though some of the men went into deep depression and could not deal with prison life, most were able to keep up their morale through "hope" and the belief that the end was near. They received books from the YMCA along with athletic equipment, musical instruments, theater equipment, etc. Touch football was a favorite, and as luck would have it both Stalags had former college athletes to add to the skill level.

As for entertainment, the *Kregies* were fortunate to have trained performers to put on theater productions. Davidson remembers that "when the guys dressed up like girls and put on the proper padding and make-up, they appeared to be beautiful girls."[19] Bolen remembers that Luft I put on a very good play, "The Man Who came to Dinner." Other *Kregies* used their various talents to help keep up morale in any way they could. Even their German captors, who faced their own bouts of depression, especially as the war turned against them, enjoyed the remarkable talent of the *Kregies*.[20] For example, on Christmas Day, 1944, Corley used his rich baritone voice to sing Christmas carols throughout the compound. As he trudged through the snow, Corley decided to sing to a camp guard. He knew enough to sing Silent Night in German and when he finished the guard replied that he understood. That incident saved Corley's life in the final hours of the "the long march" near the end of his captivity. That same soldier caught him in what appeared to be an effort to escape. As he pointed a gun at him, he recognized Corley as the one who had sung "Silent Night." Corley survived one more near death experience.[21]

Of course the most important morale booster was mail from home. But such letters were rare, and at best, the POWs could expect mail about once a month. In his ten months as a POW, Bolen received two postcards, one letter, and no packages. Four packages were returned to his family and arrived after he returned home. The letter informed him that his first child was born the week after he was shot down. He learned of that blessed event in February 1945.

To attempt to escape from the camp a POW had to go through a complicated process, and he had to present his plan to a compound escape committee. But approval for escape plans was rare, especially after the "Great Escape." In Luft I, one POW tried to escape on his own without going through the committee, and Bolen remembers that "the farthest he got was between the warning wire and the main barb wire fence. He was taken by the Germans to solitary confinement for a month." Few escapes were attempted after that.[22]

In January 1945, the war was in its final phase. The Allied forces under General Eisenhower had broken the Seigfried line while the Russians were advancing toward the Ober River. The town of Sagan, the location of Stalag Luft III, was about forty miles from the Ober in a direct line from the Russian advance and its objective, Berlin. German officials decided to move the 20,000 prisoners west, away from the advancing Russians. One of the worst periods of captivity was about to begin.

The grueling "long march", as it was called, began on the bitterly cold evening of January 27, 1945, and continued until the POWs reached the camp at Moosburg, south of Nuremberg, near the southern border of Germany. The American camp commander alerted the men a few days prior to the march and encouraged them to exercise as much as possible to prepare their bodies for the ordeals that were ahead. Fortunately, the Red Cross came through again and issued the men wool underwear, socks, trousers, jackets, caps, and overcoats, along with U.S. Army blankets and some food. Davidson believed that the preparation may have saved their lives in the terrible days ahead. At about 8:00 p.m. the German camp commandant gave the order for the POWs to be ready to march in one hour. McCaleb remembered that initially the prisoners felt some relief in leaving the barbed wire confinement of the prison camp and having the opportunity to see the German countryside. But, by the time they walked a few kilometers, already cold and exhausted, they questioned their delight at leaving the stalag. The entire march tested their endurance to the maximum as the POWs struggled against both the weather and the cruelty of some of the German guards, They faced ten-degree weather and twelve inches of snow made worse by ten-mile-per-hour wind. When they attempted to rest the German guards, assisted by yelping and snapping dogs, prodded them to either keep moving or be shot.[23]

Corley remembered the ordeal of the first night as he almost lost his life. "We marched fifty minutes of each hour and stopped ten," he remembers. "During one of the ten minute rests, I sat down on the right side of the road. I was so very tired and fell asleep and I was hit by a motorcycle of a German officer going past. When I came to, I was head down in the snow and could barely stand up because of a re- injury to my back." For Corley events only got worse. On one occasion, the column dispersed and dove for the ditches when bombers appeared overhead. As Corley lay in the ditch, feet frozen, he remembers a German sergeant attempted to encourage him to get up by sticking a bayonet a quarter of an inch into his back, ordering me to march or die. I didn't think I could march," he said, "however, somehow, I kept walking on my frozen feet. I vowed to live to get that bayonet from that fellow—and I did, the day we were liberated." He remembered helping four men who had collapsed by the side of the road get on their feet. On one occasion, a fellow prisoner attempted to escape into the woods. He and a friend tackled the man just as a guard was about to shoot him.[24]

Davidson remembered that they were urged to keep moving because the Russian army was so close to them they could hear the gunfire. "The blizzard was so bad," Davidson said, "that many men passed out and fell in the snow. Everyone was too exhausted to help them, and I am sure that many of them died." He remembered that "the Luftwaffe guards who were mostly middle-aged men and not in as good physical shape as the Kriegies also fell by the side of the road and probably died there. Horses pulling wagons of rations froze to death leaving the food by the side of the road. On one occasion, McCaleb remembered a guard too exhausted to carry his rifle. "He simply dropped it in the snow and stumbled on," he said. Davidson recalls a German Guard leaning on a bridge rail who toppled into the icy creek when the rail broke. "Everyone was too tired to help him," he said.[25]

During the long march, the men spent nights in any shelter available. Davidson spent one night on a church pew and another in a brick kiln. One night Corley remembers more than a hundred prisoners being crammed into a barn. On other occasions, the POWs spent the nights in abandoned warehouses or, on occasions, private homes. Eventually, the survivors of the march, arrived at a railroad station and were loaded into boxcars for a grueling train trip. The boxcars were of World War I vintage and were referred to by their maximum load of 40-8, meaning "forty men or eight horses." The Germans managed to cram fifty to fifty-five standing prisoners in the cars, creating miserable and very unsanitary conditions. Corley remembered that a carload of Red Cross food parcels was in one of the marshaling yards when the train stopped briefly for the men to get some fresh air. The Air Force Colonel who had been in charge of Corley's compound at Stalag Luft III talked the German guards into issuing the food to the men. Corley said "this was the first real food the men had eaten in five days and most of us ate a large part of the food right away....Most of the men had diarrhea with no facilities for hygiene except a one and one-half foot opening in the boxcar door." Davidson said that his constant fear was that the prisoners might be strafed by allied aircraft while inside the box cars. The train stopped on occasions for long periods of time and the POWs were given "some box lunch type food." Finally, after an exhausting and miserable trip, the prisoners arrived at Nuremberg and were placed in a prison camp formerly used by Italian prisoners. While the prisoners were glad to leave the train, they did not find much comfort in their new camp. Corley described the remainder of his captivity as "Hell on Earth."[26]

The Nuremberg prison camp was crowded and filthy, much worse than the men had endured in Stalag Luft III. They slept in four-deep bunk beds that were infested with fleas and bed bugs. The latrine was outside their barracks and they were not permitted to use it after 9:00 p.m. Everyone had dysentery. During the two or three weeks at Nuremberg the prisoners sweated out the frequent bombing raids, British by night and the American Eighth Air Force by day. When the bombs fell on the camp, the prisoners were herded outside the barracks into the trenches where they watched the show. On one occasion, McCaleb observed a crippled B-17 at low altitude. He remembers the scene as "the plane was hit by antiaircraft fire and exploded. Pieces of metal floated to the ground."[27]

On April 4, and fortunately in warmer weather, the men marched again, this time to Moosburg. At that time, the American army was about thirty miles from Nuremberg. As they traveled on foot, they were constantly exposed to allied aircraft strafing or bombing any target in sight. To avoid such attacks, the men marched at night. Davidson remembers stopping at a farm house where he was given two fresh eggs and boiled potatoes. Those were the first eggs he had received since October 15, 1943, the day after crashing in France. On another occasion, he raided a pig pen where he found some potatoes in a food trough. They provided a "truly tasty treat," he said.[28]

On April 18, the POWs who had left Stalag Luft III four months earlier, arrived at Moosburg where they joined some 50,000 other prisoners from every allied nation. Since the barracks were full, they were assigned to tents where they slept on the ground. While life at Moosburg was crowded and unsanitary, the time there was short. Eleven days later, at 8:00 a.m., Sunday, April 29, American tanks appeared over the crest of the hill above Moosburg and headed for the valley where the camp was located. Davidson describes the events that followed: "Our joy soon ceased,...when we saw the river bridge explode as the German SS destroyed it. Now we thought the tanks could not get across the little river near our camp. About thirty minutes later, we heard gunfire. The tanks had gone up the river and found another bridge to cross. The SS troops with only small arms had tried to fight the tanks but were soon annihilated by tank guns...At this point the Luftwaffe guards lined up and threw their guns in a pile and surrendered...As we looked toward town, we saw a German flag flying above City Hall. We saw the German flag being lowered and the Stars and Stripes go up in its place...This was such an emotional moment that it made goose bumps cover my body,"[29] "There were tears flowing down many cheeks," recalls McCaleb. "We had survived the greatest war in history."[30]

Behind the three lead tanks, another rather special tank appeared with General George Patton standing in the turret. Corley will never forget the experience of being summoned to meet the General and being quizzed as to the treatment he had received. Corley told him that "some of the guards had been fair, but one officer had stabbed him in the back. The General was ready to shoot the officer on the spot," but Corley said "there has been enough killing." Corley did get the dagger from the German as he had vowed to do during the long march.

A short time later, Patton's army brought the beleaguered men fresh bread and delicious vegetable soup with meat in it.[31] For the men of Stalag Luft III, along with the many other prisoners that had joined them at Moosburg, the war was truly over.

For Bill Thompson and Frank Bolen at Stalag Luft I, the route to freedom did not involve a long march to a different camp. Luft I, located at Barth in Northern Germany, was much further from the American and Russian advancing armies than Stalag Luft III. By the time the Russians arrived there, the war was over. On May 7, 1945, Thompson heard the distant rumblings of artillery and knew the Russians were near. On May 9, the POWs awakened to a silent camp and discovered that the Germans were gone. The Russians had begun the process of liberating the prison. The POWs were not released immediately, however. They were flown out by the Eighth Air Force only after an equal number of Russian prisoners held by the Germans were flown in. In effect, the Americans were swapped for Russian prisoners. Finally, after being interviewed by the Russians, the Americans were flown to France. In discussing the final trip out of the Stalag, Bolen tells of the one of the saddest sights he saw during the war. That was "of German people of the little city of Barth, on the day we marched through on the way to the landing field where the B-17s awaited us. The inhabitants had lined the streets to watch us march by and tears streamed down their faces as they watched us go. They realized that with the departure of the last Americans from their soil, they were at the mercy of the Russians who hated them." One more sad story in a horrible war.[32]

Bolen's observations and his ominous feelings toward the Russians reflected views shared by a number of military men in the final days of the war. No example better illustrated the reality of such views than the story of Franklin C. Pepper, a B-24 Flight Engineer with the 453rd Heavy Bombardment Group, who became a prisoner of war, not of the Germans but of America's ally, The Soviet Union. On March 15, his crew, on its 22nd mission, was to bomb the German army staff headquarters at Zossen, twenty miles south of Berlin. The bomber was well into Germany when a fire broke out on the flight deck. After extinguishing the fire all was well until the bomb run. Then, not only did a second fire break out, but the aircraft lost two engines and electricity. The Liberator quickly lost altitude and descended 10,000 feet before the pilot could gain control. Since the aircraft could no longer keep up with the formation, the pilot was ordered to attempt to fly into Poland 150 miles away and land at a Russian air base. With some luck and a great deal of pilot skill by Wes Bartlet and his copilot John Parker, the bomber eventually made it to the Russian base at Lodz. As it approached the base, Pepper fired double red flares indicating an aircraft in distress. Then the unexpected happened as two Russian fighters took off and began firing at the bomber. The fighters hit the bomber in several places including the control panels and even blew the wheel out of the pilot's hands. Bartlet remembers that his one thought was," What kind of allies are they?" The crew had no choice but to bail out even though the altitude was about 1,000 feet, too low for safe descent. Pepper and seven other crew members miraculously made it safely to the ground, but the navigator, Hans Niichel, and the tail gunner, Ken Olsen were killed in the low altitude bail out.

No sooner had the men hit the ground than Russian troops surrounded them and took them to an old barn. There they found another crew of a B-17 that had also landed at the Russian base, also as a result of being forced down by the trigger happy "allies."

For the next few days the crews were under armed guard and released from the barn only for short times for meager meals. After a few days, they were taken into Lodz where they were secured in a hotel, two men to a room. There they underwent interrogation from a KGB Colonel. The Russian Colonel, interrogated the POWs as if they were their enemy, asking for information on their bases, radio call signs etc., but Bartlet refused to answer him and reminded the unhappy Colonel that if he and his men were prisoners "they should be treated under the rules of the Geneva Convention." He later remembered that the Colonel "shook his finger at me and speaking in a loud voice said, 'You smart, young Lieutenant, in twenty-five years, we will control your country without firing a shot.'" Fortunately, after about four weeks of captivity, the Russians decided to release the airmen and took them to an air field where they were turned over to United States army personnel. They were transported by a Russian DC3 to Poltava, Russia, the only air field the Russians allowed the Americans to use. There they boarded an American transport for the trip back to England. Thus ended one of the most unusual incidents in the story of POWs, one Franklin Pepper, a farm boy from the little town of Athens, Alabama, would never forget.[33]

Cambridge American Cemetery (Photo by author)

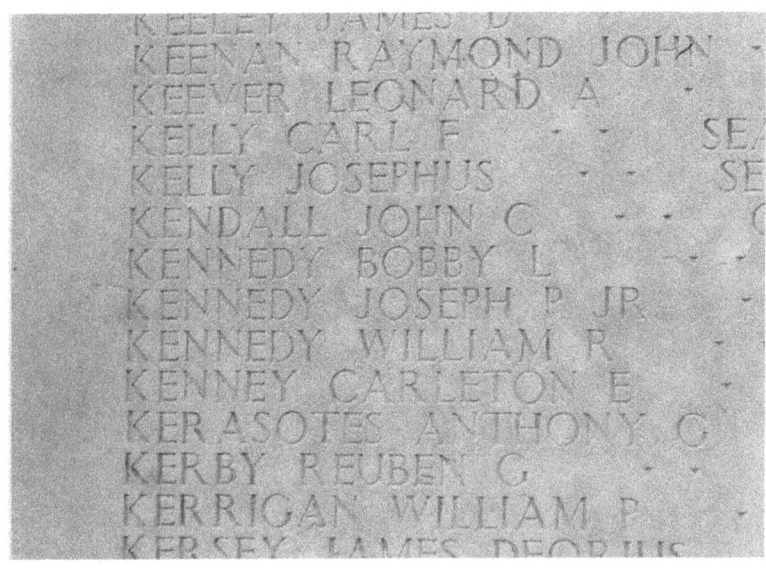

Wall of the Missing, Cambridge American Cemetery; name of Joseph P. Kennedy who was killed on Aphrodite mission
(Photo by author)

Restored control tower, Thorpe Abbotts Air Field, home of 100th Bomb Group. (Photo by author)

Ceiling of Eagle Pub, Cambridge, England. Names, symbols, units. Inscribed with burning candles by RAF and American crewmen, 1940-45. (Photo by author)

8

Over, At Last

I suppose this is the greatest day in our history.
    Noel Coward, V. E. Day

At 6:20 A.M. on April 20, 1945, the B-17 "Miss Fortune," 385th Bomb Group, took off from its base at Great Ashfield and joined some 800 heavy bombers to attack the railroad marshaling yards near Berlin. It was Bill Varnedoe's twenty-sixth and last mission. Seven days later another bomber from his Group, while flying a mercy mission to the Netherlands, was slightly damaged by flak in what may have been the last shot fired at the Eighth Air Force in World War II. Strategic bombing of Germany that began August 17, 1942, and had taken the lives of some 26,000 airmen, had come to an end. No one on that first bombing mission to France could imagine the ferocity of air combat that followed in the next 458 missions. In his diary, Varnedoe summed up in a succinct way the most often heard expression of Eighth survivors: "We had survived."[1] No longer did they have to face each day wondering if it would be their last.

For John Hard, copilot in the 100th Bomb Group, the end of the air war coincided with the completion of thirty-five missions. He recalls that he was so elated with the realization that he could finally go home, he did what so many airmen did; "he got stinking drunk." But he went one step further when he stumbled into his Quonset hut and spotted his Colt 45. "I took it outside the door," he remembers, and "pointed it up towards the sky and emptied the clip just as fast as I could pull the trigger. Then I went back in just dying laughing. I found my box of shells, loaded up again and went back outside and did it again." His celebration came to an abrupt end as a MP threatened him with arrest. "Boy, you never saw anybody sober up so fast in your life. Look, don't arrest me," I said, "I have just finished my thirty-fifth mission and am due to ship out any day to go back to my wife. He said, 'don't lie to me Lieutenant.' I said, I'm not lying, you can check at squadron headquarters. He looked at me a long time before handing me back my gun, and said, 'Go home and give your wife hell, Lieutenant.'"[2]

At Great Ashford, "we shot Very pistols (flares) in lieu of fireworks," recalls Varnedoe, "and felt very, very, happy. Unfortunately, one of those flares set a farmer's haystack on fire, but even that could not dampen our joy at the war's end."[3]

And so it went, or something like it, on all of the bomber and fighter bases in England. Disbelief that it was finally over caused everything from unabashed crying to prayers of thanksgiving, to noise and drunkenness, and in some places destruction of property. The most powerful air armada in history had done its job—and done it well! While other young men along with women would experience aerial combat in other wars in the years that followed, they would never duplicate the scenes of war forever embedded in the minds of the men of the mighty Eighth.

In the days immediately following the German surrender, many Eighth Air Force crews went back to Germany to look at a country they hardly ever saw when concentrating on hitting selected targets that were often obscured by smoke or altitude. George Owen and his B-24 crew rewarded some of his group's ground crew by giving them a low-altitude sightseeing tour over Germany. They had the opportunity to see what the aircraft they had so carefully maintained had done to Hitler's Fortress Europe. "We flew over Mannheim, Frankfort, Cologne, and other towns," Owen said, "and at one stage of the flight we flew over the Rhine River for quite a distance. All the bridges we saw were down in the water."[4]

Charles Patterson was one of several airmen in the 305th bomb Group privileged to assist in the liberation of Air Force prisoners of war. While he did not know it at the time, some of the released prisoners from his hometown of Birmingham Alabama, were among those he airlifted. Following that project, he too got a good glimpse of war-torn Germany. He recalls that "Cameras were installed in the bomb bays and, we began photographing runs of 200 miles out, and 200 miles back...This operation began in Belgium and lasted several weeks." He also remembers flying to Paris whenever he wanted to go. Like so many other veterans of the European war, Patterson expresses his gratitude, that in spite of the horrors of war, he did see much of the world he might never have seen otherwise.[5] Many American communities were to be the beneficiary of returning veterans' experiences, world view, and competency as they returned to greatly enhance their social, cultural, and political fabric.

Bill Varnedoe had a special type of humanitarian experience. Instead of carrying American prisoners of war, the 385th Bomb Group assisted in mercy missions to drop food and other supplies to the Dutch who had suffered so long in the German occupation. He tells the story at reunions of "a Dutch kid standing on a dike, waving an American flag." He remembers that his pilot came very close to making a "snap roll" in wagging his wings at the youngster. Varnedoe also went on a sight-seeing tour in which his B-17 flew low enough to see the details of the landscape. "The tour was a novelty," he said, "since all of our combat missions had been at least above 20,000 feet." He recalls the relief at no longer being distracted by flak or searching enemy fighters. "Then we could see just how destructive our bombing had been," he said. "The rubble and debris were everywhere in great piles as if the bombs had just fallen." On one trip, his B-17 was used to transport twenty-five Frenchmen home who had been forced laborers of the Germans. When the plane passed over the rubble that had been German towns, he remembered that "the French would grin, and pat us on the back when they saw what we had done to their enemy. It was certainly unmistakable how pleased they were."[6]

For the airmen who spent much of the war as POWs, the release was none too soon with every day a struggle for survival. Frank Bolen remembers how conditions in Stalag Luft I changed after February 1945 when the German Wehrmacht took over the camp replacing the Luftwaffe. Then, he states, "we were treated the same as infantrymen in the Army. They made life harder. They did not permit any fraternization between the guards and the prisoners. They had us stand in the snow for an hour at roll call…This was a particularly lean time when we did not have enough food to keep us active. Stomach pains and prostrate on the sack were the order of the day …"[7]

Etched into Lawson Corley's memory was a sobering experience a few days before air evacuation from Moosburg; a visit to the death camp at Dachau. In later years, as he talked to students and civic groups about his POW experiences, he added Dachau at the top of the list of injustices he had witnessed as an "example of man's inhumanity to mankind." Corley also had the satisfaction of visiting the beer hall where Hitler began his plans of conquest; plans that had such a lasting impact on his life and indeed the entire world.[8]

Roy Davidson sums up his reactions after General Patton released the POWs in Stalag Luft III, as ones of "happiness and rejoicing." Even the little things he had taken for granted prior to his captivity took on special meaning. After adjusting his stomach with a diet of bland food, he remembers the best meal he had ever tasted, of "fresh bread and delicious vegetable soup with meat in it." He had lost thirty-five pounds as a prisoner of war, and wasted no time in attempting to regain his lost weight. On the transport ship taking him home, he bought boxes of Hershey bars with almonds, "the first candy I had eaten in one and a half years. I ate all forty-eight bars, and did not even get sick," he said.

Davidson also recalls observing from the air the Germany he was happily leaving behind. He especially remembers that, as the cargo plane he was in flew at a low altitude, he too saw that "every town was a pile of rubble." As he looked at the war damage he remembers thinking that, "The German people were certainly paying for Hitler's inhumanity."[9]

Bill Thompson did not spend as much time in Stalag Luft I as many of the prisoners, but his three months there were long enough!

He too understood how precious freedom could be. He also missed little things. For example, he recalls that on the ship home, "all the guys were really happy and I spent most of my time in the ship's bowels listening to country and western music by the guys that had confiscated German instruments."[10]

Kenneth McCaleb was released along with Corley and Davidson from Stalag Luft III. He adds to their account with a memory of the scene on Sunday, April 29, when they were liberated by the 14th Armored division of the 3rd U.S. Army. Like most POWs the sight of the American flag flying from a church steeple was one of the most moving experiences of his life.[11]

Within a couple of weeks after the last bomber had departed, many Eighth Air Force bases that had been carved out of the plush English farm land in East Anglia and the Midlands underwent a transformation back to the pastoral landscape as it had been in 1942. While young men who came to England as "boys" began the process of returning home as "men," the original owners of the lands converted the former bases to peaceful pursuits. Although the Englishmen were happy to see the war end and pleased to repossess their land, they were sorry to see the Americans go. The gratitude remains with them today. When British residents from villages next to American air bases look back to that time, they agree with a Framlingham farm girl who remembers, "we never felt at ease until all of them (the crews) had landed. We called those boys 'our boys,' and their ships 'our ships.'"[12]

George Stebbings, who had watched the construction of Knettishell and the arrival of the planes and crews, remembers the silence when the last bomber departed in 1945. Daily, he had ridden his bike to the base, and he became a fixture with the crews, many of whom were reminded of their younger brothers at home. His recollections cause his eyes to well up and he will quickly tell any visitor that his days among the air crews were the happiest of his life, and he has nothing but appreciation for what the Americans did. When Americans visit Knettishell, he is proud to provide them with a personal tour of what remains of the 388th Bomb Group, and when asked why he devotes so much time to telling the story of the Eighth Air Force, his answer was, "After what you Americans did for us this is the least I can do."[13] That comment is echoed by many of the residents of East Anglia.

Six decades after the departure of the last bomber, Cliff Hall, who lives within a short walk of Bury St Edmunds, serves as the major contact for former airmen visiting what remains of the former base. He has the most extensive private collection of 94th Bomb Group photographs in existence, and gladly loses himself in memories, as he discusses the "greatest years of his life." He enjoys spending hours with visitors identifying crew members by name, home town, and memorable missions they flew. He is also a frequent guest at 94th Bomb Group reunions both in England and in the United States.[14]

No sooner had the war ended than weary members of the Eighth began the long awaited trip home. When Franklin Pepper returned to Old Buckenham from his brief captivity at the hands of our Soviet allies, the 453rd Bomb Group had already started moving. "As we landed," he remembered, "6x6 trucks were moving out, loaded with bomber crews and ground personnel. All were waving and hollering goodby." He joined another group and within a few days flew home in a "war weary B-17."[15]

The trip home on the B-17s and B-24s turned into an ordeal for some crews. Bill Varnedoe describes his experiences when he departed Great Ashfield in an aircraft named "Sweet Chariot." He said that like the old spiritual, "it was coming for to carry us home." The first stop was Valley Wales where he saw one more tragedy of war. "A P-51 pilot buzzed the field to salute his brother in a bomber crew, but misjudged the water at the end of the runway and crashed." The "Sweet Chariot" crew had the ominous task of swimming out to retrieve the body. From Valley he then flew to Keflavick Iceland, where the B-17 encountered both icing problems and clouds that made the landing hazardous. The next stop was at the head of a fjord on a small piece of land between water and a glacier. The bomber had one chance to land, or else hit the glacier. By using all of his skill, the pilot landed safely. Following the next leg of the trip to Goose Bay, Labrador, the worn-out bomber landed at Bradley Field, Connecticut. The crew that had experienced so much of the horror of war together said their goodbyes and then split up. Varnedoe then followed the routine experienced by so many of going home on a thirty-day leave and then to another training base, Sioux Falls, South

Dakota, where he was to train for the Pacific War. Fortunately while he was in route, Hiroshima was bombed, ending the last chapter of the long war. In October, he was discharged in time to enroll in the fall quarter at Georgia Tech.[16]

The dates of departure and mode of travel back to the States varied between those who completed their required number of missions during the war and those who finished their tour as the war ended, but most processed back to civilian life by Christmas. Henry Arnold completed his tour in April 1944 at the height of the air war feeling extremely lucky to have survived some of the worst missions of the war. Many of his friends in the 94th Bomb Group were not so lucky, a sad fact that he has never forgotten. He had defied the odds, but the sights he had witnessed from his ball turret would never leave his memory.[17]

December 7, 1941, seemed so long ago to returning veterans. They returned to the communities they left behind to find their wives, relatives and friends leaving their own war behind. They had lived a time of uncertainty, rationing, and support for a war that was so distant from their loved ones, both in miles and in understanding. They knew their friends and relatives had fought some horrific battles, but the sanitized version reported by the media left many questions as to the reality of war. Even many of the letters they received from those experiencing the war first hand had been censored. For those in POW camps, letters were often never received.

When husbands returned to wives they scarcely knew or children they had never met, transition to civilian life was not easy. When Lawson Corley, who had suffered the horrors of Stalag Luft III, returned home, he remembers a difficult time of readjustment. His wife Florence expresses a common view of many Eighth Air Force wives and family members who were kept in the dark as to what their loved ones were doing. She said: "we didn't know too much about his missions, just the number of missions, and that he could come home after twenty-five of them." And, like so many other Americans who saw the war through dark colored glasses, Florence is quick to affirm that, "wars are not just things that happened but real experiences that changed lives forever."[18]

When the airmen returned home they often found the hometown little changed from the one they left behind. Main Street, the corner drug store, the local movie theaters—all seemed so familiar in appearance, but yet they were different-or was it the veterans who had changed? In his book *Montgomery in The Good War,* Wesley Newton quotes Bill Lawrence's return home: "Home at last! Or was I home?" Everything looked the same but somehow it wasn't. Yet was it that I had changed or was it home?" When he visited his old high school Lawrence realized, "I didn't belong there anymore ... I left my boyhood somewhere on a bomb run over Germany ... No, I wasn't the same and neither was anybody else. Nor was Montgomery."[19]

In spite of their difficult experiences, the men of the Eighth Air Force took many of the qualities and skills they had gained in the service, entered the civilian work force, and often became the backbones of their community. While they would be the first to say they were not the greatest generation, few historians today can doubt that they improved the world to which they returned in profound and distinctive ways. Glenn Taylor recounts his difficulty of adjustment: "Upon discharge, I took a year to get myself unscrambled." But then he goes on to say, "I think my military experience taught values I could not have gotten otherwise. Certainly it taught me to appreciate life more." He went on to use the GI Bill to attend the University of North Carolina, where he received his degree in journalism in 1950.[20] John C. Butler returned home July 24, 1944, after his 30th mission, and used his education benefits to complete his college education, including his pharmacy degree from Samford University. Others followed a similar pattern and within a year after the conclusion of the war, most had put the war behind them, married, found employment, or entered college. Their perseverance and success were enhanced by maturity forged in the realities of war and, most significantly, they shared appreciation of the country they fought to defend.

Some airmen saw their future shaped directly by war experiences. For example, Roy Davidson decided to become a dentist as a result of an unlikely experience in Stalag Luft III. Just before his October 1943 mission to Schweinfurt that eventually caused his captivity, he had planned to have dental work done—after completing his twenty-five missions. That delay and his non-programmed incarceration left him no choice but to seek dental work in the POW camp. That experience put him on course to become a dentist. He was impressed how the two dentists, also POWs, one British and one from New Zealand, filled two of his teeth in such a painless manner. He especially remembers that "they seemed to be enjoying their work which was possible with the equipment and supplies furnished by the Red Cross." Following his discharge in 1945, Davidson became a very successful dentist in Birmingham, Alabama.[21]

Kenneth McCaleb, who shared Stalag Luft III with Davidson, resumed his education that had been interrupted in 1942 at Missouri Southern State College. After graduating with a degree in mechanical engineering, he began a career in the space program that eventually brought him to the Marshall Space Flight Center in Huntsville, Alabama. In 1998, after retiring from the space program, McCaleb and his wife Margaret, gave $150,000 in stock to the Missouri Southern Foundation for the establishment of the "McCaleb Initiative for Peace." From his personal ordeal in war, he recognized what many military men understand, that when you know war first hand, you want to do all that you can to prevent it. Through funds provided by the *Initiative* he helped student journalists at Missouri Southern, on assignment for the college newspaper, research the subject of war and peace by visiting sites of former wars, and even some sites of conflicts then in progress. Interestingly, a reporter from the college newspaper the *Chart,* with his support, attended the 1998 reunion for the survivors of the Schweinfurt mission that had made such a profound change in McCaleb's life.[22]

While many veterans from the Eighth Air Force elected to return to school or resume careers that had been interrupted by the call to arms, several remained in the military service. Bill Thompson and Bill Lawley were among those who went on to complete full careers, both retiring with the rank of Colonel. Lawley's service included a tour as aide to General Fairchild, Vice Chief of Staff, who played such an important role in organizing the new Department of the Air Force. Louis Kline also remained in the service, and along with Thompson and Lawley, served during both the Korean and Vietnam wars.

Many Eighth Air Force veterans such as John Echols of Los Angeles, California, who later made Alabama his home, remained in the Air Force Reserve, retiring after thirty-five years. John had flown on the same bomber with his twin brother Don, until the latter was wounded on his fourteenth mission over Belgium. Don went to college and completed a career with General Motors. Owen O'Rourke from Mobile, stayed in the Air Force Reserve, received a commission, and served for thirty-five years including twenty-two months on active duty during the Korean War. When Frank Bolen returned to Selma after his release as a POW, he helped form a new Army National Guard unit. Like O'Rourke, he was called to active duty in the Korean war, not as an Air Force bombardier, but as a tank commander. He served in Korea for thirteen months before being returned to civilian life.

Andrew Chaffin left Gadsden, Alabama, in 1943 as a First Lieutenant and returned there in 1945 as a Lieutenant Colonel. He had survived thirty-seven missions. But he was perhaps best known in his hometown for the unauthorized flight he took just before departure overseas. As a pilot on a B-17 en route overseas he decided to give his family and the city a spectacular farewell. The *Gadsden Times* reported that "while in a flying fortress, he dived fourteen times over the Chaffin home and dropped a box of candy and a note to his mother, coming close enough to brush the tree tops. He also laid a smoke screen down the main street. The fire and police departments of Gadsden protested the farewell and the commander of a nearby Army camp tried to have him 'busted,' but he was overseas and beyond the reach of civil and military disapproval." Needless to say, his return with numerous medals as a hero after the war, left the memories of two years earlier far behind. Chaffin continued in the Air Force, retiring after thirty-five years as a Colonel.[23]

The common denominator in the post-war lives of the Eighth Air Force veterans is the pride they have in what they did in the skies of Europe. They served because that is what they believed they should do when their country called. Even though they sacrificed precious years of their young lives, they have no regrets, and to a man they are quick to say they would do it again. Yet they do have memories that neither time nor circumstances can take from them. Those memories are often private, or if revealed, are done so in the company of other

Eighth Air Force veterans who share them, and most importantly provide understanding not available among family or others who were not there.

On August 29, 1986, 126 Alabama Eighth Air Force veterans formed a chapter of the Eighth Air Force Historical Society as a forum to share their memories and to communicate with a world that knows very little about what they did decades ago. They not only share their stories at the state level, but also at national, group, and squadron reunions, and on occasion, reunions at their former bases in England. In June 2002 one such reunion was held at Thorpe Abbotts, the former base of the 100th Bomb Group. Only forty-five veterans and their wives attended but the restored control tower was open to British citizens who lived in the vicinity of the base. They came by the hundreds to get a glimpse once again of the men who came to their neighborhood so long ago to save their way of life.

That devotion by the British of East Anglia is shared by a younger generation, who have heard the stories from their elders of the exploits of the Americans who came so long ago to be a part of their culture. They brought with them vintage automobiles and dressed in clothes from the war years. To the familiar strains of Glenn Miller music they relived a bygone era, and when a P-51 buzzed the restored control tower, both they, and the aging warriors, were reminded of a time when such flights were not always friendly. Several British spectators, caught up in the emotions of the moment, wiped tears from their eyes. As is so often the case at such reunions, some of the veterans found a few moments to go out to the deserted runway, now mostly a wheat field, to lose themselves in memories. Once again, they are young, and "their thoughts focus on never forgotten faces of so many young men who took off from that field never to return." The reunions are not just for the living.[24]

Veterans who attend such reunions or visit England usually make one more crucial stop before leaving England. They travel to the Cambridge American Military Cemetery, located three miles west of Cambridge. The thirty-acre site was donated by Cambridge University on December 7, 1943, to become a permanent American military cemetery as a memorial to the Americans who fought and died while stationed in England. The site was chosen not only because of scenic grandeur of the area, but also as a location on the edge of East Anglia, home of so many Eighth Air Force bases. At the cemetery entrance is a seventy-two foot flagpole with the American flag and its clanging chain making the only noise other than that of the birds and a few rustling leaves. The Eighth Air Force veterans have difficulty describing their emotions as they move along the "Great Mall" that stretches eastward toward the memorial. Its beauty is enhanced by reflecting pools and a dense cover of Polyantha roses. Parallel to the mall is the 472 foot "Wall of the Missing." There, among the 5,125 names of missing Americans whose remains were never recovered or identified, are names from every bomb group. Then, across from the mall are rows and rows of white crosses above grave sites of 3,812 Americans. While the average visitor sees names and homes of record, the Eighth Air Force veteran sees much more. They were young men who were "brothers" in war. They arose from their slumber on cold British mornings just as thousands of others, and took to the air to complete one more mission that turned out to be their last. The thoughts that linger in veterans' minds are, "what they might have become," and the realization, that for reasons they will never fully understand, they went and died while "I" survived. Then as the veterans enter the memorial chapel at the east end of the mall, they read the following words of tribute around the perimeter of the mosaic ceiling: *In proud and grateful memory of those men of the U.S. Army Air Force who from these friendly skies flew their final flight and met their God. They knew not the hour or the day, nor the manner of their passing, when far from home they were called to join the heroic band of airmen who had gone before. May they rest in peace."*

NOTES

Chapter 1 — December 7, 1941: Lives at the Crossroads

1. *Montgomery Advertiser,* December 6, 1941.

2. Wesley Newton, *Montgomery in the Good War: Portrait of a Southern City 1939-46* (Tuscaloosa: University of Alabama Press, 2000), 46.

3. Diana Polin, letter to Donald E. Wilson, April 23, 2001, Eighth Air Force Collection, Samford University Library, SUV.

4. Dora Hill, letter to Wilson, May 22, 2001, SUV.

5. Frank Bolen, autobiography, Eighth Air Force Collection, Samford University Library, SUV.

6. Amy Arnold, letter to Wilson, June 1, 2001, SUV.

7. Dora Hill, letter to Wilson.

8. Joy O'Rourke, letter to Wilson, April 14, 2001, SUV.

9. *Birmingham News,* December 9, 1941; *Honolulu Star-Bulletin, December 7 and 8, 1941.*

10. *Cullman Tribune,* December 18, 1941.

11. Ibid.

12. Lawson Corley, interview by Wilson, Jan. 29, 2002, SUV.

13. *Birmingham News,* December 8, 1941.

14. *Limestone Democrat,* December 11, 1941; *Cullman Tribune,* December 26, 1941.

15. *Birmingham News,* December 13, 1941.

16. *Montgomery Advertiser,* December 8, 1941.

17. *Fayette City Times,* December 25, 1941.

18. *Birmingham News,* December 8, 1941.

19. *Montgomery Advertiser,* December 24, 1941.

20. Ibid., December 29.

21. *Birmingham News,* December 29, 1941.

22. Ibid., December 28.

23. Wesley Frank Craven and James Lea Cate, *The Army Air Forces in World War II,* vol. I, (Washington, D.C.: Office of Air Force History), 2.

24. Charles Shinault, letter to Wilson, April 17, 2001, SUV.

25. William Holcombe, letter to Wilson, April 3, 2001.

26. Raymond Hill, letter to Wilson, May 22, 2001.

27. Louis Kline, letter to Wilson, April 13, 2002.

28. Glenn Taylor, letter to Wilson, March 24, 2001.

29. John Hard, letter to Wilson, June 13, 2003.

30. Ibid.

31. Lawson Corley, interview by Wilson.

32. Roy Davidson, autobiography, Eighth Air Force collection, SUV.

33. Amy Lawley, letter to Wilson, March 22, 2001, SUV.

34. Bill Massey, letter to Wilson, March 26, 2001, SUV.

Chapter 2 — What was the Eighth Air Force?

1. Glenn Taylor, letter to Wilson, March 24, 2001, SUV.

2. Ibid.

3. Charles Jones Jr. file, Eighth Air Force collection, SUV.

4. William Mitchell, *Winged Defense: The Development and Possibilities of Modern Air Power—Economic and Military,* 255.

5. Wesley Frank Craven and James Lea Cate, *The Army Air Forces in World War II,* vol. I, 51-52.

6. General Donald Wilson oral history, AFHRC.

7. Sebastian Cox, Introduction to *The Strategic Air War Against Germany,* 7-8; and Introduction to *Dispatch On War Operations, 23rd February, 1942, to 8th May, 1942.*

8. Frank Bolen autobiography, SUV.

9. Asa N. Duncan, letter to Chief of Staff, Army Air Force, Feb 12, 1942, Charles Jones Jr. file, SUV.

144

    10. Craven and Cate, vol. I, 590-591.

    11. Edward Jablonski, *Flying Fortress,* 86.

Chapter 3 — Two Cultures, A Single Objective

    1. George Stebbings, interviews by Wilson, July 16, 1997 and April 10, 1995, Knettishell, UK.

    2. Ron Batley, interviews by Wilson, January 1999 and June 2002, Thorpe Abbotts, UK.

    3. Stebbings, interview by Wilson, April 10, 1995.

    4. *British Heritage,* August-September 2000; Donald E. Wilson, *On The Trail Of Patriots In World War Two Britain,* 31-35.

    5. William Dupree, letter to Wilson, undated.

    6. Harry Crosby, *A Wing and A Prayer,* 32.

    7. *British Heritage,* May 1997.

    8. Sam Hurry, interview by Wilson, April 11, 1995, Thorpe Abbotts, UK.

    9. C.B. Harper, *Buffalo Gal,* 48-51.

    10. Howard Polin, letter to Wilson, April 23, 2001.

    11. Guy Coffield, letter to Wilson, April 25, 2001.

    12. Gerald Astor, *The Mighty Eighth,* 14.

    13. Benton White, memoir, Eighth Air Force Collection, SUV.

    14. Quitman Hurdle, memoir, letter to Wilson, April 17, 2000, Eighth Air Force Collection; Lawson Corley, interview by Wilson, June 11, 2001, SUV.

    15. Harper, 47-53.

    16. Ibid.

    17. Walter Fleming, letter to Wilson, March 20, 2001, SUV.

    18. Harper, 53-55.

    19. Ibid.

    20. Ibid.

    21. Samuel Ross, autobiography, Eighth Air Force collection, SUV

22. White, memoirs.

23. *Over There, Instructions for American Servicemen in Britain, 1942,* 1-3.

24. Stebbings interview.

25. Hall, interview.

26. Bill Sharpe, interview by Wilson, Atcham UK.

27. Hilburn Richards, letter to Wilson, April 24, 200, SUV.

28. Bolen, autobiography.

29. Gardner, 53.

30. Ibid.

31. Glen Taylor, letter to Wilson.

32. Cofield letter to Wilson.

33. Charles Gay, letter to Wilson, March 23, 2000.

34. Ritchie, letter to Wilson.

35. Polin, letter to Wilson.

36. Gardner, 8637. Polin, letter to author.

37. Polin, letter to Wilson

38. Bill Varnedoe, letter to Wilson, March 2001, SUV.

39. Polin, letter to Wilson.

40. *Over There,* 11.

41. Stebbings, interview by Wilson.

42. Monthly Report, 94th Bomb Group file, AFHRC.

43. Ibid.

44. Red Cross Report, 94th Bomb Group file, AFHRC.

45. Ibid.

45. *Over There*, 8.

46. Gay, letter to Wilson.

47. Taylor, letter to Wilson.

48. Bolin, letter to Wilson.

49. Hard, letter to Wilson.

50. Ibid.

51. Fleming, letter to Wilson.

52. Dupree memoirs, Eighth Air Force Collection, SUV.

Chapter 4 — An Uncertain Beginning

1. Craven and Cate, vol. II, 306-308, 665-669.
2. *Strategic Air War Against Germany*, 11.
3. Craven and Cate, vol. II, 308-309.
4. Howard Abney, letter to Wilson, May 5, 2001, SUV.
5. Walter Boyne, *Clash of Wings,* 197-205.
6. Ibid.
7. Louis Kline, letter to Wilson, SUV.
8. Chronology, 145.
9. Kline, letter to Wilson.
10. Ibid.
11. Craven and Cate, vol. II, 665-669.
12. Ibid. 708.
13. Chronology, 145, 149-150.
14. Abney, letter to Wilson.
15. Chronology, 163-177.
16. *Birmingham News,* August 19, 1943.
17. Kenneth McCaleb, letter to Wilson, May 1, 2001.
18. *Strategic Air war Against Germany*, 8-9.
19. Crosby, 92.
20. Craven and Cate, vol. II, 685.
21. Kline, letter to Wilson.
22. Astor, 147-49.
23. Kline, letter to Wilson.

24. Abney, letter to Wilson.

25. McCaleb, letter to Wilson.

26. Brian D. O'Neal, *Half A Wing, Three Engines and a Prayer,* 51-56.

27. Kline, letter to Wilson.

28. Ibid.

29. McCaleb, letter to Wilson.

Chapter 5 — Darkness of Winter, Light of Spring

1. Roy Davidson autobiography, Eighth Air Force collection, SUV.

2. Ibid.

3. Davidson, autobiography.

4. Craven and Cate, II, 702.

5. Ibid.

6. McCaleb, letter to Wilson.7. Davidson, autobiography

7. Davidson, autobiography.

8. Williamson Murray, *Luftwaffe,* 216.

9. Ibid.

10. Craven and Cate, II, 705.

11. Henry Arnold, letter to Wilson.

12. Ibid; Mission Report #106 and statistical Summary of Missions, December 1943, AFHRC.

13. Ibid; Arnold, letter to Wilson.

14. Amy Lawley, letter to Wilson.

15. Arnold, letter to Wilson.

16. Ibid.

17. Harper, 87-93 and History of 100th Bomb Group, 91.

18. Crosby, 202.

Chapter 6 — Air Superiority

1. *Birmingham News,* June 6, 1944.

2. Boyne, 330-341; Craven and Cate, vol. II, 370.

3. Murray, 258-259.

4. Corley, interview by Wilson, and enclosed documents, Eighth Air Force collection, SUV.

5. Craven and Cate, vol. III, 186-194; Stephen Ambrose, 93-96.

6. Ambrose, 239; John C. Butler, letter to Wilson, April 14, 2001.

7. Taylor, letter to Wilson; White, letter to Wilson.

8. Polen, letter to Wilson.

9. Taylor, letter to Wilson.

10. Tom Winslett, letter to Wilson.

11. Polin, letter to Wilson.

12. Murray, 268.

13. Craven and Cate, vol. III, 278-279.

14. Boyne, 349.

15. Chronology, 366.

16. Bill Massey, letter to Wilson, March 26, 2001, SUV..

17. Ben White, memoirs, SUV; History of the 94th Bomb group.

18. Walter Fleming, letter to Wilson.

19. Raymond Hill, letter to Wilson.

20. Bolen, autobiography.

21. Hard, letter to Wilson.

22. Vernedoe, letter to Wilson.

23. Ibid.

24. Craven and Cate, 725; David Mets, *Master of Airpower, General Carl A. Spaatz,* 268-273.

25. *Eyes of the Eighth,* 155-58.

26. Charles Shinault, letter to Wilson, video interview, April 1, 2001, SUV.

27. Craven and Cate, 727-28; Aphrodite Mission Summary, 1944/45 SUV.

28. Chronology, 571-72; Craven and Cate, 728.

29. Hill, letter to Wilson.

30. Mets, 275-276.

31. Craven and Cate, 735.

32. Ibid. 719.

33. Varnedoe, letter to Wilson.

34. William Holcombe, letter to Wilson.

35. Bill Thompson, letter to Wilson.

36. Owen O'Rourke, letter to Wilson.

37. Varnedoe, letter toWilson. Varnedoe learned 60 years later that the Gerrman pilot had survived the mid-air collision.

38. George Owen, letter to Wilson.

39. Paterson, interview by author, April 3, 2003, SUV.

Chapter 7 — Evasion, Capture and the Stalag

1. Bolen, autobiography.

2. Corley, interview by Wilson.

3. Bolen; McCaleb letters to the Wilson.

4. Bolen, autobiography.

5. Corley, interview by Wilson, Jan. 2, 2002, SUV.

6. McCaleb, letter to Wilson.

7. Roy Davidson, autobiography; Davidson, interview by Wilson, April, 2003, SUV.

8. Corley, interview by Wilson.

9. Bill Thompson letter to author.

10 Ibid.

11. Davidson, autobiography; quote from POW Thomas P.

Griffen, 82-3.

12. Bolen, autobiography.
13. Ibid.
14. Thompson, letter to Wilson, March 17, 2001, SUV.
15. Bolen, autobiography.
16. Thompson, letter to Wilson.
17. McCaleb, letter to Wilson.
18. Thompson, letter to Wilson.
19. Davidson, autobiography.
20. Bolen, autobiography.
21. Corley, interview by Wilson.
22. Bolen, autobiography.
23, McCaleb, letter to Wilson; Davidson, autobiography.
24. Corley, interview by Wilson.
25. McCaleb, letter to Wilson; Davidson, autobiography.
26. Corley, letter to Wilson; Davidson, autobiography.
27. McCaleb, letter to Wilson.
28. Davidson, autobiography.
29. Ibid.
30. McCaleb, letter to Wilson
31. Corley, letter to Wilson.
32. Thompson, letter to Wilson; Bolen, autobiography.
33. Franklin Pepper, video interview to Wilson, April 26, 2001, SUV.

Chapter 8 — Over At Last

1. Bill Varnedoe, letter to Wilson.
2. John Hard, letter to Wilson.
3. Varnedoe, letter to Wilson.

4. George Owen, letter to Wilson.

5. Paterson, interview by Wilson.

6. Varnedoe, letter to Wilson.

7. Bolen, autobiography.

8. Corley, interview by Wilson.

9. Davidson, autobiography.

10. Thompson, letter to Wilson.

11. McCaleb letter to author.

12. Rex Allen Smith, *One Last Look,* 81.

13. George Stebbings, interview by Wilson.

14. Hall, interview by Wilson.

15. Pepper, video interview.

16. Varnedoe, letter to Wilson.

17. Arnold, letter to Wilson.

18. Florence Corley, letter to Wilson, June 11, 2001, SUV.

19. Wesley Newton, *Montgomery In The Good War,* quotes Bill Lawrence.

20. Taylor, letter to Wilson; Butler, letter to Wilson.

21. Davidson, autobiography.

22. McCaleb, letter to Wilson.

23. *Gadsden Times.*

24. Observations of Wilson, June 2002.

Bibliography

Astor, Gerald. *The Mighty Eighth: The Air War in Europe as Told by the Men who Fought It.* New York: Donald Fine Books, 1997

Ambrose, Stephen E. *D-Day, June 6, 1944: The Climatic Battle of World War II.* New York: Simon & Schuster, 1994.

Barksdale, Jerry. *When Duty Called.* Athens, Al.: Magnolia Press, 1998.

Boyne, Walter J. *Clash of Wings.* New York: Simon and Schuster, 1997.

British Bombing Survey Unit. *The Strategic Air War Against Germany, 1939–1945.* London: Frank Cass, 1998.

Carleson, Lewis H. *We Were Each Others Prisoners.* New York: Perseus Books, 1997.

Clodfelter, Mark. *The Limits of Air Power.* New York: Free Press, 1989.

Combat Chronology, 1941-45. Compiled by Kit Carson and Robert Mueller. Washington, D.C.: Center for Air Force History, 1991.

Craven, Wesley Frank, and James Lea Cate, eds., *The Army Air Forces in World War II,* vols 1-3. Chicago: University of Chicago, 1979.

Crosby, Harry. *Wing and a Prayer.* New York: Harper, 1993.

Freeman, Roger A. *The Mighty Eighth.* London: McDonald, 1970.

Gardner, Juliet. *Overpaid, Oversexed, and Overhear:* New York: Canopy Books, 1992.

Harris, Sir Arthur. *Bomber Offensive,* London: Collins, 1947.

Homan, Lynn M. and Reilly, Thomas. *Tuskegee Airmen.* Gretna, La.: Pelican, 2002.

Jablonski, Edward. *Flying Fortress.* New York: Doubleday, 1965.

Kaplin, Phillip and Currie, Jack. *Round the Clock.* New York: Random House, 1993.

Keen, Patricia Fusell. *Eyes of the Eighth.* Sun City, Az: CAVU, 1996.

Le Strange, Richard, assisted by James R. Brown, *Century Bombers: The Story of the Bloody Hundreth.* Aylsham, Norfolk, England: Rounce and Wortley Ltd.,1997.

MacIsaac, David. *Strategic Bombing in World War II.* New York: Garland, 1976.

Mets, David R. *Master of Airpower, General Carl A. Spaatz,* Novato Cal: Presidio Press, 1988.

Middlebrook, Martin. *The Schweinfurt Regensburg Mission.* London: Penguin, 1983.

Miller, Donald L. *Masters of the Air: America's Bomber Boys who Fought the Air War Against Nazi Germany.* New York: Simon & Schuster, 2006.

Mitchell, William. *Winged Defense.* New York: Putnam, 1925.

Mosier, John. *The Blitzkrieg Myth.* New York: Harper Collins,

2003.

Murray, Williamson. *Luftwaffe*. Baltimore: Nautical & Aviation Publishing Co., 1985.

Niellands, Robin. *The Bomber War*. New York: Overlook, 2001.

Newton, Wesley Phillips. *Montgomery in the Good War: Portrait of a Southern City, 1939-46*. Tuscaloosa, Ala.: University of Alabama Press, 2000.

O'Neill. *Half a Wing, Three Engines and a Prayer*. New York: McGraw-Hill, 1999.

Over There, Instructions for American Servicemen in Britain, 1942. University of Oxford, Bodleian Library, 1994.

Rust, Jenn G. *Eighth Air Force Story*. Terra Haute: Sunshine House, 1978.

Sherry, Michael S. *The Rise of American Air Power*. New Haven: Yale University Press, 1987.

Wilson, Donald E. *On the Trail of Patriots in World War Two Britain*. Birmingham, Ala: Samford University Press, 1999.

Newspapers and Magazines
Birmingham News, Dec. 6, 7, 8, 13, 28, 1941, Aug. 19, 1943,
British Heritage, April-May, 1997 and Aug-Sept. 2000.
Cullman Tribune, Dec. 18, 1941.
Fayette City Times, Dec. 25, 1941.
Honolulu Star-Bulletin, Dec. 7, 8, 1941
Limestone Democrat, Dec 11, 1941
Montgomery Advertiser, Dec 6, 8, 24, 1941

Eighth Air Force Veterans

Veteran	Bomber Groups	Location
Howard L. Abney	303rd BG	Molesworth
Henry S. Arnold	94th BG	Bury St. Edmunds
William H. Arnold	Base Airlift Depot 1	Burtonwood
Charles D. Beard	96thBG	Snetterton Heath
Frank S. Bolen	91st BG	Bassingbourne
Clyde W. Beasley	303rd BG	Molesworth
John C. Butler	453rd BG	Old Buckingham
Andrew A. Chaffin	96th BG	Snetterton Heath
Guy B. Cofield	379th BG	Kimbolton
H. Lawson Corley	446th BG	Bungay
William (Bill) Currie	357th FG	Leiston
Roy G. Davidson	94th BG	Bury St. Edmunds
William E. Dupree	448th BG	Seething
Don E. Echols	458th BG	Horsham
John E. Echols	458th BG	Horsham
Lifford E. French	381st BG	Ridgewell
Walter H. Fleming	487th BG	Lavingham
Charles L, Gay	305th BG	Chelveston
John W. Hard	100th BG	Thorpe Abbotts
John Heatherly	15th AF	Italy
William O. Holcombe Jr.	305th BG	Chelveston
Raymond D. Hill	305th BG	Chelveston
Charles A. Jones III	315 TC	
Kline Louis	379th BG	Kimbolton
William R. Lawley	305th BG	Chelveston
Burrell Ellison	392nd BG	Wendling
C.B. (Red) Harper	100th BG	Thorpe Abbotts
William A. Legg	PRS 9th AF	France
William E. Massey	401st BG	Deenethorpe
Glenn Matson	458th BG	Horsham
Kenneth H. McCaleb	306th BG	Thurleigh
John Nixon	493rd BG	Debach
Owen S. O'Rourke	457th BG	Glatton
George W. Owen	466th BG	Attlebridge

Franklin Pepper	453rd BG	Old Buckingham
Charles Patterson	305th BG	Chelveston
Howard Polin	352nd BG	Bodney
Quilla Reed	91^{stt} BG	Bassingbourne
Hilburn F. Richards	406th BS	Cheddington
James I. Ritchie	447th BG	Rattlesden
Samuel Ross	384th FG	Grafton Underwood
George A. Reynolds	458th BG	Horsham
Charles Shunault	96th BG, 466th BG	Attlebridge
Bill E. Thompson	100th BG	Thorpe Abbotts
Jasper J. Valenti	306th BG	Thurleigh
William W. Varnedoe, Jr.	385th BG	Great Ashfield
Ben White	94th BG	Bury St. Edmunds
Roger D. Welk	381st BG	Ridgewell
Thomas E. Winslett	448th BG	Seething

Other Contributors

Family Members of Veterans
Amy Arnold
Henry S. Arnold, Jr.
Virginia Abney
Frances Bolen Atcham
Florence Corley
Martha Lanis Currie
Dora Hill
Claradel S. Holcombe
Amy Lawley
Margaret McCaleb
Diana Polin
Joy O'Rourke

British Friends
Ron Batley, Thorpe Abbots
Cliff Hall, Bury St Edmunds
Sam Hurry, Thorpe Abbots
Bill Sharpe,

George Stebbings, Knettishell

INDEX

Abney, Howard L., 54, 59
Air Corps Tactical School, 18-19, 21
Air War Plans Division, AWPD-1, 24
Ambruster, Clark, 97
American Red Cross, 46-47
Anderson, Frederick L., 61-62
Aphrodite, 98-99
Arcadia Conference, 24
area bombing. *See* terror bombing,
Army Air forces, U.S. (USAAF), 8
Army Air Service, U.S., 15
Arnold, Amy, 3, 57, 101
Arnold Henry H. "Hap," 8, 15, 23, 57,69,74-76, 79-80
Arnold, Henry S., 3, 76-77, 79-81
around the clock bombing. *See* Combined Bomber Offensive
Barth, *See* Stalag Luft I
Bartlet, Wesley, 128-129
Batley, Ronald, 30
Battle of Britain, 22
Battle of the bulge, 121
Beard, Francis L., 93
Berlin
  as target, 101
Big Week, 78-79
Birmingham News, 5-7, 86-87, 132
Boeing B-17 Flying Fortress, 11, 19-21, 28
Bolen, Frank, 3, 24, 41-42, 107-8, 110-12, 118-19, 124, 128-29, 134
Bolen, Frances, 3, 95, 107-8
Bolero, Operation, 25
Brereton, Lewis H., 75-76
British Air Staff, 61
British American Relations, 40-45
Brookley Field, Alabama, 6
Brzones, Donald, 119
Bury St. Edmunds, 46-47
Butler, John C., 88, 137
Casablanca Directive, 52
Chaffin, Andrew A., 139
Chichester, Stan, 74
Churchill, Winston
  bombing policy, 1, 23-24, 52-53
Clarion, 100-1
Cofield, Guy, 34, 43
combat chronology, 19, 41-45,
Combined Bomber Offensive Pointblank, 59, 61, 76
Combined Strategic Targets Committee (CSTC), 100-101
Coney Weston Anglican Church, 47

Congressional Medal of
  Honor, 79
Consolidate B-24 Liberator,
  11
Corley, Florence, 136
Corley, H. Lawson, 5, 11-12,
  35, 81, 88, 110, 112, 117,
  119, 124, 125, 133, 136
Coward, Noel, 130
Craig Air Corps Training
  Base, 6
Craven, W.F., and J.L. Cate,
  *The Army Air Forces in
  World War II*, 63, 64
Crosby, Harry H., *Wing and
  a Prayer, 32, 63, 82-83*
D-Day, 25, 31, 86-90
Davidson, Roy G., 12, 39,
  68-73, 112-20, 122, 133,
  137-38
DeWeerdt, Paul, 103-04
Dickens, Charles, 39
Doolittle, James H., 15, 32
Donitz, Karl, 55
Dresden, bombing of, 23
Duncan, Asa, 8, 15-16, 26-
  27, 106
Dupree, William, E., 32, 50
Eagle pub, Cambridge, 48
Eaker, Ira, 15, 18, 21, 27-28,
  52, 54, 57, 59, 68-69
East Anglia, 29-30
  air fields, 20-33
Echols, Donald E., 129
Echols, John E., 138
Eighth Air Force, U.S., 86,
  88, 98
  activation, 25, 30

aerial tours of Germany,
  1945, 131-133
arrival in England, 27-28
bases, 27-33
Bomber Command, 55
organization changes, 75-
  76
Eighth Air Force Historical
  Society, 25, 139-140
Eisenhower, Dwight D., 27,
  100-1
  Overlord, 87, 88, 91
Eisenhower, John, 88
European Theater of
  Operations (ETOUSA)
Fairchild, 138
Faudie, Al., 113
Fayette County Times, 7
Federal Bureau of
  Investigation, 5
Fifteenth Air Force, 31, 59,
  75-76, 86, 92
Fighter Planes, U.S.
  and D-Day, 90
  P-38 Lightening, 74
  P-47 Thunderbolt, 23, 74
  P-51 Mustang, 23, 74
Fighter Planes, German, 70
  Focke-Wulf FW 189, 55
  Messerschmitt ME 109,
    20, 53-56, 59, 61,
  Messerschmitt ME BF
    262
Fleming, Walter H. 37, 50,
  94-96
French Underground, 113-15
Fuchida, Mitsuo, 2
Gay, Charles L., 43, 48

Geneva Convention, 116, 129
Gestapo, 112, 116-17
G-men, 5
Goebbels, Joseph
and Terrorfliegors, 111
Goering, Hermann, 25
Great Britain, 18
Great Escape, 123
Griffen, Thomas P., 119
Grosvnor House, 44
Gunners, bomber, 76
Gunter Field, Montgomery, Alabama, 6
Hamburg, 23
Hard, John W., 10-11, 48, 97-99, 131
Harper C.B. (Red), 34-38, 81-82
Harris, Arthur Sir, 21-23, 53- 54, 91
"Hells Angels," 54-55
High Wycombe, 27
Hitler, Adolph, 25
Hill, Dora, 4
Hill, Raymond S., 10, 100
Himler, Henrich, 111
Holcombe, William O. Jr., 9, 102-3
Honolulu Star Bulletin, 4
Hurdle, Quitman, 33
Hurry, Sam, 33
Keesler Field, Mississippi, 9
Kennedy, Joseph. *See* Aphrodite

Kline, Louis, 10, 54-57, 59, 63, 138
Kruger, Frederick, 113-14, 116
Lancester, Avro, bomber, 21
Lawley, William Jr., 12, 78-80, 138
Lawrence, William, 137
Lay, Bernard, 65
Leigh-Mallory, Sir Trafford, 27, 86
LeMay, Curtis E.
and 100th Bomb Group, 62
London
air crew leaves, 44
V-1 and V-2
"Long March," 123-126
Luftwaffe
losses, 54, 59, 68-74, 83, 90-91
and Normandy invasion, 54, 68-91
McCaleb, Kenneth H., 60-72, 112, 126, 133, 138
McDill Air Force Base, Florida, 9
Madingly Military Cemetery at Cambridge, 140-41
Massey, William E., 12, 93, 94
Maxwell Field, Montgomery Alabama, 6, 11
Midland bomber sites, 31
Mitchell, William "Billy,"
and concepts of air power, 17-18

court martial, 16-17
Winged Defense, 17
Moosburg
  and POWs, 133
Mungenasst, Richard, 113
National Defense Act of
  1945, 18
Newton, Wesley, 3
Niespodziewany, Walter, 87,
  112
Niichel, Hans, 128
Ninth Air Force, U.S., 31,
  66, 68, 75, 92, 95
Norden bombsight, 21
Nuremburg
  and POWs, 125-27
Oil, German, 87, 92, 94, 98
Olsen, Kenneth, 128
O'Rourke, Joy, 4
O'Rourke, Owen S., 4, 103,
  138-39,
Overlord. *See* D-Day
  preparations for, 76
observation from the air, 86
Owen, George W., 105, 131-
  32
Paine, Thomas, 39
Patterson, Charles, 132
Patton, George S., 127
Pepper, Franklin C., 128-29,
  135
Pilsen, Czechoslovakia 16
Pinetree, 27
Pointblank, *see* Combined
  Bomber Offensive
Polin, Diana, 3
Polin, Howard, 34, 44, 89-90
Portal Sir Charles, 76

Prisoners of war (POWs)
  as Terrorfliegers, 111
  confinement locations,
    110
  life as, 110, 119-21
  statistics, 109-10
  railroad targets. *See*
    Transportation Plan
  rationing, 7
Regensburg, 52, 59-65
Richards, Hilburn F., 41
Ritchie, James, 43
Rockets *see* V-1, V-2
Ross, Samuel, 29, 38-39
Roosevelt, Franklin D., 4, 8,
  24
Rouen-Sotteville, France, 16,
  51
Royal Air Force (RAF), 18,
  74, 98
  Bomber Command, 53,
    86, 88
  and U-Boats, 55
Schweinfurt, 52, 59-65, 68-
  74, 112
"Sea Lion," 25-26
Sharp, William, 41
Shinault, Charles, 9, 99
SHAEF (Supreme
  Headquarters Allied
  Expeditionary Force),
  100-1
Smith, James, 90
Soviet Union
  advance into Germany,
    127-29
  treatment of downed
    airmen, 128-29

Spaatz, Carl A, "Tooey" 15, 27, 51, 74, 66, 91, 98-100
Stalag Luft I, 24, 104-12
Stalag Luft III, 87, 110, 112-14, 119, 124,
Stebbings, George, 30, 40-41, 134-35
Stelljes, Lewis V., 93
Strategic Air War Against Germany, 74-75, 77
Target priorities, 52
Taylor, Glenn, 10, 12-16, 42, 88-90, 138
Tedder, Sir Arthur, 86
Terror bombing, 22-23, 97-99
Thompson, Bill E., 103-4, 118-27, 133, 138
Thorpe Abbotts, 32-33, 37-38, 140
"Torch," (North Africa), 54-55, 58
Transportation Plan, 87-81
Trenchard, Hugh, 17
"Trident," (Italy), 54
Turner Air Force Base, Georgia, 11
U-Boats (submarines), 52, 55, 57-58
ULTRA code intercepts, 90
U.S. Army Air Forces tactical and fighter bomber groups
   91st Bomb Group, 24, 41
   93rd, Bomb Group, 92
   94th Bomb Group, 70, 76, 89, 93, 136
   96th Bomb Group, 58, 99
   97th Bomb Group, 51
   100th Bomb Group, 32, 37-38, 48, 60-72, 81-82, 95, 118
   303rd Bomb Group, 54, 56, 64-72
   305th Bomb Group, 60-67, 71, 105
   338th Bomb Group, 30
   352nd Bomb group, 34
   379th Bomb Group, 34, 43, 54, 58
   381st Bomb Group, 44, 97
   384th Bomb Group, 29, 38, 135
   385th Bomb Group, 44, 96, 97, 130
   388th Bomb Group, 30
   401st Bomb Group, 92-93
   406th Bomb Group, 105
   447th Bomb Group, 43
   448th Bomb Group, 32, 90
   457th Bomb Group, 104
   466th Bomb Group, 15, 42, 88
   487th Bomb group, 33, 50, 94-95
   492nd Bomb Group, 41
   4th Fighter Group, 55
V-1, (Vengence Weapon; buzz bomb), 91-92
V-2, 91

Varnedoe, William W. Jr.,
  44-45, 96-97, 101-2, 104-5,
  130-31, 135-36
White, Benton, 35, 39, 89,
  93-94
Winn, Eugene, 87
Winslett, Thomas E., 90
Zeppelins, World War I, 16

ABOUT THE AUTHOR

DONALD E. WILSON is Professor of History Emeritus, Samford University, where he taught and specialized in military history. He is also retired from a career in the U.S. Air Force, where his assignments included among others, five years on the history faculty at the Air Force Academy, and several assignments at the Air University. His life-long interest in Air Force history and specifically the Eighth Air Force was enhanced by assignment to the Air Force Historical Research Center, Maxwell Air Force Base. In addition to several articles and book reviews, he previously published a book, *On the Trail of Patriots in World War Two Britain*. He resides in Birmingham, Alabama.

www.ingramcontent.com/pod-product-compliance
Lightning Source LLC
Chambersburg PA
CBHW070917180426
43192CB00037B/1651